I HAVE SOME THINGS TO TELL YOU

A PASTOR SAYS GOODBYE DURING A PANDEMIC

JENNY SMITH

CONTENTS

DEDICATION

For the ridiculously kind and gracious people of Marysville United Methodist Church in Washington State. You cheered me on when you had no idea how desperately I needed a cheering section.

Thank you, forever, for that gift.

INTRODUCTION

"We're moving. During a pandemic. And I can't see our people?"

Several months ago, I got the call saying it was time to serve at another church. As itinerant pastors, we say yes to serving faith communities one year at a time. Yet, the call to move is still a disruption. Like a rocket exploding on the 4th of July, many feelings burst forth from my existence. I felt sad, curious, disappointed, excited, and called. But the one causing me the most grief was this thought: *How will I ever thank my Marysville family for what they gave me?* Each time the thought flitted through my head, tears welled up.

March arrived. Headlines grew urgent. School stopped. We were told to stay home. Fear hung in the air. A global pandemic was upon us.

A few weeks into quarantine, I received an email saying a publishing house did not want to publish a book proposal on palms up that I'd worked on for two years. I felt relieved. I also felt a little embarrassment, good old fashioned rejection, and sadness. I expected the last three, but relief? Upon further reflection, I unearthed a curious thought.

Maybe palms up isn't ready to become a book. I spent a few hours wondering what to do with the tumbling grief of saying goodbye during a pandemic. Then it hit me.

What if I wrote a book to my church?

There's so much I want to tell them. And we're in a pandemic. Quarantined for weeks, possibly months. And Lord knows I'm carrying a lot of grief and loss these days. Maybe writing a book to my church is one way I can invite my grief to flow down my cheeks and onto these pages.

I mean, it's either write the book or pack up the house, right? Yeah, I'm going to write a book.

I set aside time each morning to write, remember, celebrate, and cry. I went through multiple boxes of tissues as I pulled together journal entries, sermons, funny quotes from my kids, poetry, and new essays. As I got to the end and wrote a few specific letters to people, I realized something.

Yes, this book is for the people of Marysville United Methodist Church.

It's for me, too. It's the story of reckoning with fear until it offers gifts of freedom on the other side.

Consider this your invitation to be a fly on the wall as these stories unfold. May something here spark a new question in your life. I'm glad you're here!

To my Marysville family, since we literally cannot stand within six feet of each other or exchange a hug or see each other's tears or share an inside joke, this is my gift to you. This is my way of saying with unending gratitude from the bottom of my heart, thank you. Church, I hope the stories of these pages show you the gift you give your pastors. May these stories shed light on God's movement in this community. May you laugh along with the innocence of young hearts and the honest questions from a heart trying to find its home. May these pages ahead show you the soul of a pastor who has loved you dearly and wants to joyfully release you to meet, support, and eventually love your new pastor.

This is a bizarre transition. Using a bizarre tool, like a pastor writing a book to say goodbye during quarantine feels appropriate.

During one of the early days of quarantine, I found myself crying over the losses piling up. Instead of crying alone, I went downstairs to hug my husband. Our two children came around the corner and typically I would brush away the tears and move on. But this time, I couldn't. The kids curled up in my lap. I told them I felt sad. We pulled out my phone and looked at pictures from our last five years in Marysville. Tears continued to roll down my cheeks while we laughed and told funny stories.

At that moment, I brought my grief into our family space. Instead of hiding away in silence and embarrassment, my tears were accepted. Normalized. And wow, did I feel so much lighter. Bringing these stories to you is one small way to normalize grief. We each face loss, especially during a global pandemic. Let's be people who show up with our full selves in this world. It's all welcome.

Thank you, publishing house, for saying no. It wasn't the right time. I imagine palms up will have its day. But that day isn't today. And maybe you even knew there was something else I needed to write first. Here we go.

THERE WAS MORE GOING ON

I t would have been easy to leave Marysville and never tell you this story. Especially during a pandemic. I could have sent you a video goodbye and skipped town.

But there are some things I have to tell you.

The story you hold in these pages centers around the five years I served as your Lead Pastor from 2015-2020. I joined you with some extra baggage I hoped to hide well.

How It Started | July 10, 2015

My mom tells stories of my stomach aches before school many mornings. I desperately wanted to please people in charge. My teacher, my parents, school administration. I remember being ever so vigilant to ensure people noticed me doing good. Adults needed to see my creative science fair project on the acidity of orange juice. I chased the smile and encouragement from my music teacher as I learned how to play percussion in our 5th grade band class.

Their approval was my life force. It gave me breath. I couldn't relax without it.

It never occurred to me as a young child that this was unhealthy or abnormal. My brain didn't know I could question this way of being in the world. It was so much a part of me that I couldn't separate any conscious intention from the desperate desire for approval.

I don't remember anxiety being a big thing throughout junior high and high school. I had the normal challenges of feeling uncomfortable in my changing body and figuring out how to relate to boys when I liked them but they were oblivious of my existence. Normal teenage drama and angst. First boyfriends entered the scene in high school and it was still the same drama and angst. Nothing earth shattering. I learned a lot about myself, my boundaries and how to love someone. The break ups were awful and those tears simultaneously broke my heart and put it back together. But I wasn't anxious.

College was a blast. I loved the independence. I still can't believe I only applied to one school in Florida and ended up being there for four fantastic years. Flying back and forth from Alaska to Florida several times a year got old. But I loved walking to class and passing the palm trees, sand and swimming pools. We drove to the beach on the weekends and changed clothes three times a day because of the humidity.

It was halfway through college that something started to turn. I met this guy. My heart knew something was different this time. He was patient, funny and calm. Everything I was not. We were friends for a year before we started to look at each other differently. Was there something more here?

Our chaplain at the time gave Aaron $20 and encouraged him to take me on a date. Others saw our connection before we did. I remember flying home for Christmas two months after we started dating and my parents asked about him and I said, "I'm going to marry him." They were surprised, to say the least. But the heart knows when it finds something real.

Our conversations turned more serious by the month. We both knew we'd already decided this was a forever thing.

The fear started to whisper. But I never heard it. It started as symptoms. And being a Type A self-diagnosed hypochondriac, I fixated on symptoms like a hawk.

Back in high school, I remember trying out for our varsity volleyball team my senior year. I had played club volleyball that summer to prepare and I felt ready. The first day of tryouts came. I ran, hit, dove, and scrambled my way around the gym that day. I remember looking around and thinking I had a pretty good shot at making the team.

By the end of the day, my arms hurt so much. More than I thought they would. I drove home and went right to my bedroom. Tears rolled down my cheeks as my arms throbbed with pain. "What if I can't do this?" I hoped the next day would be better. I came home the second day and my arms were even worse. It felt different than just sore muscles. It got so bad, I had to quit tryouts. I remember coming home and collapsing on my pink flowered bedspread in my room. The cheeriness of my room taunted my pain. It was my senior year of high school and I knew I couldn't play volleyball this year. I threw the pity party of the year that day.

My mom was an elementary school nurse at the time and dragged me around to doctor after doctor after doctor when each one didn't know what it was. I did physical therapy, took supplements, tried different medications and stretches. I eventually had to quit playing piano for our school's production and percussion for my school band. Finally, someone mentioned fibromyalgia. Everything fell into place. Isn't it funny how having a word to cling to in an uncertain season grants so much comfort, even if it's not anything you ever wanted.

Fibromyalgia taught me that I couldn't trust my body. It betrayed me at the age of 17. I couldn't control it. To make it worse, most other 17-year-olds were thinking about prom, chemistry homework and the next football game. My friends didn't understand why I couldn't do everything they wanted to do.

When the symptoms started to shift in college, they scared me. I was getting used to how my fibromyalgia would react to stress in life. It never occurred to me that the symptoms were from anxiety. They were simply symptoms that felt terrifying.

Those cross-country flights between home and college became restrictive and scary. I would panic at different moments in the travel day. The nerves and fear in the transitions to and from school become debilitating.

I remember one specific night before getting on a late flight out of Alaska. My family had dinner together. These were always intriguing as we tried to cram a semester's worth of conversations into an hour. Mom made the lasagna I loved but my stomach was twisted up in knots. My younger siblings danced between sentiments they would miss me and getting last-minute digs in. I found myself packing up a few last minute things in my room. A growing sense of dread rose. The tears slipped out my eyes as I sank into the corner of my closet. Maybe if I just stayed in here, I wouldn't have to get back on a plane. This back and forth between my childhood and my growing up was slowly destroying me.

I walked into my parents' room and sat on the edge of their bed. My dad sat down next to me as I cried. He put his strong arm around me and pain had permission to exit my body. I loved my independence and I was terrified to grow up. I was mostly afraid of the dread.

I got on the plane that night and still felt afraid. I was so anxious that I remember freaking out about something and needing to breathe into a paper bag. The stewardess eventually had me come up front and hooked me up to an oxygen tank for a while. Looking back, I'm mortified to think of how embarrassing that was. But at the time, I was so scared of the energy in my body.

I was afraid of the fear.

It felt out of my control. It felt like I was taking my dog on a walk and we were skipping along the path with joy. And then, all of a sudden, the dog took off with me dragging behind. I didn't know why. I just knew I wasn't in control anymore of the fear. It was trying to tell me something and I had no idea I could listen to it. The fear created symptoms in my body that took my breath away with panic. I set about covering it up to the very best of my ability. I made a weird truce with the fear. "I don't know why I feel all these things, but I'm fully committed to no one ever knowing."

I did such a good job hiding my anxiety that even I forgot it was hiding at times.

I settled into college and things felt fairly comfortable. I was falling in love. And he was on board with me becoming a pastor. I was living in Florida. Life was great.

He proposed. I said yes. A wedding was planned. We promised each other forever a year later. It was beautiful. We climbed into his red truck and waved goodbye to our people. We rounded the corner of the parking lot to head to our hotel and I burst into tears. I was very aware at that moment I was leaving my family of origin. My new husband and I were young. I was about to turn 23. He was already 23. It was just us. And this poor guy was no match for what was about to be unleashed in my life. His love couldn't hold a light (yet) to the fear that had been quietly festering below the surface of my life. A foreboding sense of dread emerged as I took an official step away from what I knew to what I was equally excited and terrified of.

As we settled into our new life together, I tried my best to do all the good things a new wife does. I decorated our new little 900 square foot rental home on Merritt Island in Florida. It was my dream come true! Two miles from the Atlantic Ocean! We got a little dog from the pound. I rolled my eyes at the pizza rolls and soda he wanted to buy at the grocery store. "We're not in college anymore!" I teased as I poked his arm. We made new friends and had people over to our new home.

Our church hosted a pumpkin patch that fall. I was all in for any fall activity where we could pretend it wasn't 85 degrees in October. Aaron was in charge of the patch that year so I signed up for a bunch of shifts to help out. There were some stressful circumstances in our church that fall and the anxiety that had been waiting in the wings started to poke its' head out from behind the curtain. New symptoms caught me by surprise. One night, they got so bad that I called a friend and she took me to the emergency room. I didn't know what was happening to me and Aaron was at that dumb pumpkin patch! I remember sitting in the waiting room feeling incredibly uncomfortable and incredibly judgmental toward myself. "Look around you, Jenny. All these people are actually having real problems." They summoned me back to the room and ran a bunch of tests. They even gave me a hospital bracelet and checked me in. A little while later they sent me home and said it was nothing.

Nothing.

How could something so physically and emotionally damaging never show on a hospital test?

Why couldn't I just pull it together and be chill?

Why was I able to succeed in some parts of my life and be at a total loss in others?

I didn't have a single answer. But my awareness was rising that this was not going to be a sustainable way to live my life. I went home and framed that hospital bracelet with the words, "be still and know that I am God."

The One who made me was ever so quietly whispering my name. I was so busy playing with kids, hanging out with youth, teaching them about faith, writing Bible studies and thinking about seminary to listen to this persistent whisper.

I was too busy keeping up with my one person show. It was a full-time job. Somehow in my brain, it made sense that if I was perfect then I could outrun the fear. My truce with fear continued.

"I don't know why I feel all these things, but I'm fully committed to no one ever knowing."

Several years later, I found myself a proud owner of a Master of Divinity degree. I had mastered divinity and it was time to become "a pastor."

Our car was packed. The tent was ready. Snacks purchased. We said our goodbyes to Aaron's family in Ohio as we pointed our car toward the west coast. It was time to move to Alaska together. The decision to serve a church in Alaska had been difficult. Aaron hated to leave his family. I hated to be away from my family. One day he relented and decided to wrap his mind around being okay with Alaska. It was a tense season for us.

Moving day arrived. One last set of hugs. My husband's family choked back tears and my heart broke.

We stopped to get gas and I noticed my husband softly crying as he put gas in the car. I felt devastated. I didn't yet have the emotional ability to witness his pain and let it be present between us. I scrambled to remind him how great it would be and kept talking, talking, talking. I knew I couldn't fix this for someone I loved but I sure thought my incessant talking would soothe my nerves. Poor guy.

Looking back, I so wish I could have whispered, "I'm sorry. I'm with you." Instead, I tried to dismiss and convince away his sadness.

Thus began a very difficult drive west. This move was a larger metaphor of what was happening in my world. With each state line we crossed, I was getting closer and closer to my family of origin. This felt like home and I knew something was brewing. I couldn't put my finger on it at the time. But my spirit knew what was about to happen. This move to Alaska was about to place me in a space where I couldn't avoid this anxiety for much longer. It was about to get much worse before it got better.

I was an utter mess on this trip. Every single day my body experienced an anxiety that frustrated my husband as he tried to be supportive but didn't fully understand. We stayed at hotels where I curled up under the covers and could hardly function. He was trying so hard to enjoy this trip and my spirit was wound so tight that sleep was the only relief.

We arrived in Washington State where I was scheduled to deliver the Young People's Address to the Pacific Northwest Annual Conference. I remember walking into the room full of people and taking a deep breath. I've got this. And somehow, I did. I got up there and shared a message about planting seeds and encouraging these leaders to continue the incredible work they were doing in the world. It was working, even when fruit didn't come on their timeline.

I was commissioned an elder in the United Methodist Church that week. Given authority to offer people the grace of the communion table, the healing waters of baptism, to join two people in love and help families say goodbye to their loved ones. It was a big responsibility for anyone. But for a young woman racked with anxiety, it was a lot. I didn't even know how to reconcile what was happening in my life. But yet again, I was able to compartmentalize like a pro. I was so committed to no one knowing how scared I was, that this was like the ultimate test. I knew I was called to be a pastor so I walked down that road with courage. My fear nipped at my heels like an annoying dog but I kept moving forward. The fear was trying to get my attention, but I was too busy saying yes to God in every other area of my life. The fear was so built into the lining of my life that I didn't even recognize it as something that could be transformed.

I thought that's how life was.

Aaron and I said goodbye to our families who had flown out to be with me for commissioning. We gathered up our beagle, Zoe, into our black Ford Escape and we hit the road again. This time, heading north to Alaska.

We were in Alaska for five years where we served three churches and had two children before getting the call to come to Washington. While in Alaska, several years of therapy led to increasing realizations of how deep fear ran in my life. But I continued to compartmentalize the fear from my profession. I knew something was unfolding but was not ready to give it my full attention. Fear knows how to get loud when we don't listen, as I would come to learn in the years ahead.

Fast forward to this past January. My friend, Kate, and I were scheduled to present a talk on collaboration at The Lead Conference in Seattle. Plans changed and Kate wasn't able to participate. As much as I tried to write a talk on collaboration, it wasn't flowing. I thought about dropping out. Turns out, there was something else I needed to say.

The Lead Conference | January 13, 2020

I used to have panic attacks while preaching.

They were awful. I powered through a message about love and joy while my insides screamed at me to get out of the room. I was in fight or flight mode but had chosen, somewhere along the way, to never ever allow anyone to know there was a problem. It worked great for everyone else until I finally hit the wall one Sunday. I chose to stop my sermon, took a deep breath and told my traditional service folks I was struggling. I hung my head, with tears running down my cheeks and felt like a failure. All of a sudden I felt a couple of hands on my shoulders. Seven or eight folks had walked up front to pray for me. When they finished I gave a weak smile and said, "I don't know if I can finish my sermon." An 82-year-old woman in the second row said, "Oh, we got our sermon for the day."

It was a significant moment for a tightly wound recovering perfectionist with higher standards for myself than anyone else could ever touch. I learned that day my people wanted me and my heart, not just what I could produce for them as their pastor. They wanted me. And that continues to be terrifying and vulnerable and the best thing that ever happened to my life as a leader.

The problem is, I didn't have a class in seminary where I learned it was okay to be myself with the people in my church. I was taught...professional distance. Ethics, boundaries, authority. Those are all necessary and important things. But as I moved in different circles at school and in our denomination, I also picked up unspoken rules about competition, comparison, cynicism, and isolation.

It took a decade or so, but I realized for my resurrection work, I had to root out the sources of competition and comparison in my soul that were slowly killing me. As healing goes, what we give to God to heal inside ourselves, so often wants to heal outside of us, too.

I picked up unspoken rules about overwork, burnout, and pushing through at all costs. This collided with a fibromyalgia diagnosis I received at 17 years old. Fatigued muscles and chronic pain have taught me the dance between limits and expansion. For the last two decades I dug deep to figure out how to be well enough to keep saying yes to God's invitations. I learned to question assumptions on overwork and lack of boundaries.

I don't need this shadow leadership vibe, these unspoken rules, on top of the other stuff tripping me up in ministry. I decided to do something about it. We started a leadership cohort last summer. There are seven of us. Two serve as church planters and five serve as established church pastors. We met monthly via video, left each other video messages, texted funny memes on Sunday mornings, and rearranged our schedules to spend 24 hours together at an AirBnb this past fall. Those 24 hours were some of the most meaningful ministry I'd been a part of all year. Sitting around a fire or the kitchen counter with people I used to see as competition was water to a parched soul. Turns out Brené Brown, famed social researcher, is right. People are hard to hate close up. And not that I hated any of them. I sure was trained to hold colleagues at a safe distance. Just like I couldn't let my people see my panic, I was under strict orders from someone, somewhere to never let my guard down.

I let my guard down. Turns out we're all a little scared. Not sure what to do. We think everyone else got a playbook and our copy never showed up. We're leading in a time where all bets are off. Not much "works" that used to work. And a lot of us are dying inside of overwhelm, overwork, lack of real connection all the while nodding and smiling, "everything's fine."

I call BS.

I've stumbled into something that's saving me and it might serve you too.

Ten years ago I met someone many of you might know. Dr. Elaine Heath. I had graduated five months prior from seminary and found myself at my first pastoral appointment in Alaska. Elaine gave a keynote speech and I wrote down everything she said. Elaine shared about a contemplative stance she practiced and my heart zeroed in.

Then I read Bob Goff's "Love Does" a year or two later. He shares a great story about telling his clients in depositions to open their hands, palms up, under the table. It's impossible to feel defensive when your hands are open. The position of our body reflects the position of our heart. Bob said he'd kick people under the table if he saw their hands close up in fear. Palms up, huh? A good preacher knows a decent phrase when they see one. I preached it a couple of times. And it stuck.

Then, somewhere along the line, I combined palms up with Elaine's contemplative stance and it took on a new life of its own. This rhythm has saved me. It's become the very lifeblood of how I love, live, and lead. And it has given me the spirit with which to collaborate in fierce ways. Maybe it could serve you too.

The rhythm goes like this: *Show up, pay attention, cooperate with God, release the outcome.*

We show up just as we are to the situations and people in front of us. Mess and all. We don't apologize for it. We just show up.

We pay attention to the person in front of us and the headlines we'd rather ignore. We notice what's going on and what's not being said.

Then we cooperate with God. God is already at work in the people we know. We're not taking God to people. We notice where God's already at work and we cooperate with the Spirit's movement. This takes the pressure off of us. We're not doing this thing, God is.

Then we release the outcome. This might be the hardest part. And it will change you the most. We let go of needing to know or force outcomes. We let the situation play out. We trust that God is holding it, and that's enough. We want to give God room to work, instead of marching in with our agenda.

Palms up.

It's saving me in three specific ways lately.

Practicing a palms up rhythm has changed how I relate to my

colleagues. We put together a district retreat a year or so ago and called it "Stories of the Pastorhood." I spoke first and named my stories of competition, comparison, cynicism, and isolation. Then we spent the day talking about our relationships with each other, the distance that separates us, and where we'd like to make some shifts. We ended with an open mic session where one by one, people stood and finished this statement, "if you really knew me, you would know..." As voices cracked, tears fell and smiles warmed the room, all my competition, became human. Now when I see them, the first thing I see is their courage, their humanity and their local church struggles that all too often match mine. We really are in this together. God gets more room to work because we're learning to see and trust Spirit in each other.

Practicing a palms up rhythm has changed everything in my local church. When I first arrived, I didn't know what to preach yet so I started with what I knew. Palms up. Over the last four and a half years, it became our discipleship pathway. It is how we follow Jesus together. We've memorized the four steps and more importantly, I'm watching it take root in our own lives. So much of disciple-making feels like throwing spaghetti against the wall to see what sticks. Empowering our folks with this contemplative stance has brought more discipleship fruit than just about any other "strategy" I've tried. This crew is learning to notice and follow Spirit. This church wants to birth ten new expressions of faith in the next thirty years. I credit the ability for that vision to emerge to palms up (and to moving to a single board governance model). Palms up is helping us give God more room to work.

Practicing a palms up rhythm is saving me as a human being. There was a moment almost three years ago when I chose to stop hiding from how bad my fear and anxiety had become. I wanted to be a good pastor, a good mom, a good wife, and a good leader and I finally owned up to the truth that I couldn't get there while pretending I had it together anymore. Living a palms up life gave me the structure and the courage to keep going a little bit deeper inside my heart. Each time, I was scared of what I might find, but I kept finding more beauty. More love. More of the Divine. Freedom. Hours with a therapist, spiritual director, coach, trusted friends, and loved ones continue to lead me closer and closer to who I am and the me I've covered up with a million expectations, assumptions, and pain.

My beloved friends, may we be people who move through life with open palms. May we surrender control over people and plans. May we learn to let go of agendas and manipulation and fear. May we be leaders who dance in the truth that the pressure is off. The rule book has been thrown out. We know we're not in charge anymore. We've given our lives to listen to the One who will take us where we need to go. And it turns out, it's where we wanted to go the whole time.

Amen.

3

FIRST IMPRESSIONS

Getting the Call I February 12, 2015

I remember getting the call from a District Superintendent in 2015. I'd been told I might be getting a call in January or February of that year. I was currently serving as Associate Pastor at St. John United Methodist Church in Anchorage, Alaska. Aaron and I had two children, Isabella and Wesley. Wesley was four months old at the time. We were sleep-deprived. I was back to work from maternity leave and it was the middle of a dark and cold Alaskan winter.

I was sitting on the floor playing with three-year-old Isabella when my cell phone rang. I jumped, saw the unfamiliar Washington state number, gave Aaron a quick nod, sprinted for our bedroom, and closed the door. After exchanging helloes, the District Superintendent told me about Marysville. I took notes and started to form images of you in my mind. I remember running downstairs to open a laptop so I could pull up Google Maps. I typed in Marysville, Washington, and saw the water and the mountains nearby. My heart skipped. Once again, the invitation to serve people near a body of water was being offered. I could hardly believe it. I feel deeply connected to Spirit when I'm by the water. My walks around the Everett Marina, Kayak Point, the Ebey Waterfront trail, the Bellingham and LaConner waterfronts have been a deep breath to my weary soul.

We scheduled a time for us to fly to Marysville to meet the Staff Parish Relations Team, see the parsonage, and visit the town. We ended the call. I flew back upstairs and breathlessly relayed the entire call to Aaron. We wrote down our follow up questions and committed to prayer for a few days. We chatted with our parents and those closest to us. Was it time? Was I ready to serve as a lead pastor? Even with two little kids? My heart screamed yes.

We met Kim and Kass, representatives from the Staff Parish Relations Team, in the church parking lot one February day. Our visit was highly confidential so it was quite a mix of feelings for this 33-year-old preacher who also needed her now five-month-old son to chill out in the back seat while I tried to make a good first impression. I wondered inside. *Would they see me as a legitimate senior pastor? I mean, I'm thirty-three. I'm still breastfeeding. I feel scared and anxious but also ridiculously alive at the possibility that these leadership gifts God placed in me are about to find a welcome home. This would be the wildest experiment of my life so far. Could I bring together all these skills and lessons I'd been honing for years and lead a group of people?*

I took a deep breath and stuck out my hand to greet them. Kass enveloped me in a hug. I could feel her love and true welcome in an instant. My spirit relaxed. We carried Wesley inside as they gave Aaron and I a quick tour around the building. There was a group of youth meeting for a weekend retreat and they were not yet allowed to see us so we looked around quickly and then hopped in the car. Kim and Kass drove us around Marysville so we could get the lay of the land. We headed to Morris & Jan's home to meet the rest of the Staff Parish Relations Team. I'll never forget walking into their beautiful home, with Wesley in my arms, and coming face to face with twelve or so very curious people. Talk about expectations colliding in that holy moment.

I wonder what this pastor is like?

What if we don't like something important to her?

She seems young. Are we sure this is a good idea?

How am I going to remember all these people's names?

What if they don't like me?

What if my son cries and I panic and look like an exhausted mom?

We enjoyed a beautiful brunch and made small talk. Then we gathered in the living room. Our District Superintendent got us started with introductions. They asked me questions. I asked them questions. It felt like a super awkward group date. But not even a date. More like an arranged marriage conversation between parents.

There comes a moment in every Staff Parish Relations Team introduction, where the incoming pastor steps out so the District Superintendent can speak to the committee about their discernment. Do you see any red flags? Does this feel like a good fit for everyone? While they had that conversation, I went to nurse Wesley. Aaron and I let out a deep breath and chatted for a few minutes about our swirling emotions. Are we all in? Is this a place where we feel called to be in ministry for a season? Is this a good fit for our children? The answer was a resounding yes in our hearts.

When we all finished up, the District Superintendent then asked the same questions of me. Any red flags? Is this a good fit? Aaron and I looked at each other and down at Wesley who was smiling in my arms. "Yes, it's a great fit. We're excited to be a part of this church family." The District Superintendent smiled and we entered the living room again.

He announced, "Friends, I'm excited to introduce you to your new pastor!" Cheers and smiles filled the room. We exchanged hugs and received lots of offers to babysit. We talked logistics of the move from Alaska and the next steps in Marysville. After another round of hugs, we walked out the kitchen door and breathed a big sigh of relief. *Marysville, here we come.*

<hr />

Isabella: "Mom, why are you sad?"

Me: "I'm sad about leaving our friends in Alaska."

Isabella: "We'll be happy in Washington."

Me: "Yes, we will. It's also sad to leave friends."

Isabella: "Their moms and dads will make them feel better...or doctors."

<hr />

First Letter to Marysville United Methodist Church | June 2, 2015

Friends! I'll be with you in just under a month. How are you feeling about that? You've said goodbye to Pastor Gloria. I just spent two days with her and I'm very thankful for her ministry among you. She's done incredible work that I'm honored to continue.

Now comes several weeks of waiting and wondering what's next. If you're anything like me, you'd prefer to skip this part. Waiting can feel uncomfortable. But as you're likely learning, God shapes us in the wait.

My three-and-a-half-year-old daughter asks me every couple of days when we're going to Washington. She's quite excited to pack her bag and hop on the plane for her new adventure. My nine-month-old is focused on learning to stand and grabbing any toy in sight. I know he'll love the home you're preparing for us. My husband is finishing up five years at his IT job and packing up our home. He'll drive the U-Haul and our car down with his parents and a friend.

What do the next couple of weeks look like for me? Our church is hosting Alaska's Annual Conference this weekend and then I'll spend a week at camp with 7-12th graders. I'll preach my last sermon at St. John on June 14. I'll say goodbye to people I've known for 16 years. It's a big goodbye. But I want you to know I've worked hard on this good-bye. I tried to feel all the big feelings and not push them away. Even when they came on airplanes, during bedtime stories, in worship, in the car or at a restaurant with a friend. These people have loved me well. They've taught me how to be a pastor. I hope you'll be grateful for their work.

I want to say goodbye well because I want to be truly ready to say hello to you. I want my heart to be open and ready for all you have to give. Here's to the transition. I invite you to pray for my family and me. We will pray for you. Hope to see you in worship in July, my friends! The adventure begins...

Your fellow disciple,

Pastor Jenny

My First Days | July 10, 2015

On my first day of work, I pulled into the parking lot and chose the spot next to the cross and the front door. I took the key out of the ignition and leaned against the backrest. *Was I really about to do this? I think I'm excited. I know I'm terrified. What if I can't do this?* Oh well, here we go.

I walked through the front door and into the office. I had stopped by a couple of days earlier to meet people and get a sense of the building.

Today was the first day to settle in and begin my work. After a conversation with our office administrator, I closed my door and took a few deep breaths.

A package on the desk caught my eye. Opening it gave me quite a surprise. It was a small photo book from a friend. Someone I'd been encouraging in ministry the last few years. She included pictures of our time together in Alaska and encouragement for this new role. I burst into tears.

Thank you, God. I'm in a new place. A new home. A new office. And people are looking at me like I'm in charge. I'm in but this is new. And I can't find myself yet in all this.

Thank you for giving me a familiar voice in this new space to help me build the bridge. Yes, we can do this. If you're here too, then I'll be fine.

I walked out to my car at the end of the day and sat in the front seat flipping through the book again. Tears warmed my cheeks as I gave thanks for transitions. That day, I set down the former and picked up the new. It would be bumpy. It would be a while before it felt comfortable and known. But best of all, God was with me and us all.

How we enter and exit spaces means something. Are we bringing our true selves in the midst of being the professional the job requires? Are we positioning our hearts so we're ready to serve?

A year or two earlier, I had a Skype session with Rev. Karen Oliveto, when she was pastor at Glide in San Francisco. I asked how she stayed grounded in her challenging role. I'll never forget her answer: "Every day, as I enter the building, I leave my ego at the door. This work is not about me."

Ever since, when I walk under the covered sidewalk entering the Marysville building, a voice pipes up inside that whispers, "This isn't about me today. Low ego."

That prayer alone made all the difference for the conversations, people, and challenges I welcomed every single day. Wow, did I learn so much in this role. When I think back to what I understood walking in that first day and what I know now about leadership in the local church, I will forever thank Marysville for the safety net you gave me.

Church, you raised me.

Thank you.

 Me: "What do you want to be when you get older?"

Isabella: "I want to teach."

Me: "What do you want to teach?"

Isabella: "I want to teach people about love."

Me: "Who do you know that does that?"

Isabella: "You."

Thank You | August 20, 2015

I'm sitting by the water in Everett, next to the marina. Listening to the small waves, the birds, a couple of cars driving by. The smell of the water makes me feel alive. The quiet beckons me like a small whisper. God, you call me. You're always calling me. I feel I've been listening more in the last several months. What are you calling me to? What kind of leader do you want me to be? How do I balance the call to make space for more people without buying into the hurry-fast-be cool and cutting edge syndrome? I want to be proactive and intentional and calm as we grow. Show me how.

Thank you, thank you, thank you for preparing me for this work. I always hoped something was coming that would so perfectly fit what you've already done in my life. I never imagined it would be this great.

Thank you for sending me to this place at this time. I will continue to focus and do everything I can to make space for others to know you.

Grace | September 18, 2015

Grace. I'm going to spend the rest of my life trying to understand and more importantly, receive grace. God, you gave us Jesus. Your word of grace. And I still don't get it. I try to earn it. Prove I can please you. If I work hard enough people will like me, and I'll be a good person. I want to be loved. Why do I resist the love people give me?

Do I think I'm not worth it?

Grace is the deepest sigh of relief possible. I want to feel the burden lift. Of trying to prove anything. I can't love others for very long if I'm not receiving your love and grace. Why do you keep speaking through my life when I don't get it? You're amazing.

The constant praise from these first two months have mostly fed my shadow side of leadership. My desire to impress people. And it's only made me work harder and harder so they'll always be impressed. This is bizarre because I'm still nursing and have decent boundaries but when I'm working, my spirit feels frantic and chaotic.

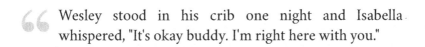 Wesley stood in his crib one night and Isabella whispered, "It's okay buddy. I'm right here with you."

A Sermon on the First Anniversary of the Marysville-Pilchuck High School Shooting | October 24, 2015

A year ago, fear, pain, terror, and grief visited this community. I watched events unfold from my home in Alaska, about a place I'd never heard of, Marysville, Washington. I remember tears streaming down my face as I imagined this community of people coming to terms with what was happening. In the past several months, I've heard your stories about this day.

"A safe space wasn't safe anymore."

"Deep sadness more than anything."

"I feel helpless."

You did what people of faith do. Gather, pray, light candles, cry, bake cookies, and open your arms to the community.

I wish this community didn't have to feel the pain they've felt in the last year. Anger, frustration, confusion, sadness. But it has come. And we each get the choice every day. Will we show up and pay attention to the hurt and pain in our world? Will we sit with it in prayer, in spirit, in presence, and allow ourselves to feel some of it, therefore, becoming part of the healing? Or will we construct elaborate walls of avoidance and fear that keep us from discomfort?

More often than not, I don't want to feel other people's pain. It's awful. My own life, pain, and fear keeps me busy enough. The thought of entering into someone else's is just too much some days. And yet, this is what we do. As the body of Christ. It's like communion. Jesus takes bread, blesses it, breaks it, and gives it to his friends. When we sign up for this discipleship thing, this is what we get to be a part of.

Jesus blesses us: Jesus gives us our identity. We are first and foremost, above everything else, children of God.

Jesus breaks us: We allow ourselves to be moved by someone else's experience. This is compassion.

There's a phrase you'll hear in our home a surprising amount. "It's okay to cry." Feelings are meant to be felt and released. We heal when we let them out. When I sense frustration, confusion, or a nervous spirit in my three-year-old, I lean down and whisper, "Isabella, it's okay to cry." The floodgates open. Her tired little body melts into sobs.

Sometimes we're so afraid of being broken by other people's grief that we avoid it altogether. Jesus continually invites us to be moved with compassion. "Blessed are those who mourn, for they will be comforted (Matthew 5:4)."

Jesus gives us away: This is the beautiful paradox of the kingdom of God. When we enter into someone else's pain, God works through us to bring healing and wholeness.

Today we pray for people like Scott. People who've walked right into fear, anger, and grief. They've been present with people in tangible and practical ways for the last year. Scott and others have been the bread of Christ broken for Marysville-Pilchuck High School. Today we pray for every individual who took a moment of care and compassion. To listen to a scared teenager, send a small gift, light a candle, support a first responder, to love those we don't understand. And most of all, we pray for the families of those who were lost. For their overwhelming moments of sadness, for the small ways they are moving on and for God to bring moments of joy into their lives.

How will Jesus give you away? For some, this means being a part of conversations around gun control. Your faith compels you. For others, you'll write a note to a staff member at the high school. For some, you'll speak to your children about how they deal with their feelings. For others, you'll drop to your knees tonight and pray.

Church, may we continue to be a people who claim our identity as children of a God who has deep compassion for all of humanity. May we allow God to break us with the things that break the heart of God. And may Jesus give us away. To be voices of great hope that peace and wholeness and resurrection are not only possible but a reality that we are seeing in our own lives. To Marysville-Pilchuck High School, we stand with you this weekend. We remember. We hope and work for a more peaceful world. May God's kingdom come.

Amen.

 "Mom, you're the best mom ever. You always bring what I need on trips!"

— WESLEY

No Longer A Nursing Mom | December 12, 2015

And just like that, I'm no longer a nursing mom. I sat down with my son in the rocking chair in the corner of his room on Sunday, December 6, and snuggled him close. I thought back to all the relaxing and weird places I've fed my kids. A Chuck E. Cheese bathroom stall, the airplane middle seat, the bunk bed at my parents' cabin, my office in between worship services, and sitting on the beach. Sometimes up to eight times a day, I would sneak off to a quiet spot and get these moments with my children. Sometimes they were painful, boring, and difficult. Most of the time they were a great reminder to slow down and pause.

I've spent a total of 30 months of my life feeding my two kids in this way. 15 months with each of them. I'm okay to be done. It's time. It's sad and it's good.

I won't miss pumping at work or on airplanes, rushing home from a meeting to nurse him, or the inability to be away from him for longer than four hours at a time.

I Have Some Things to Tell You

I don't have anything profound to say about this transition in my life. There are plenty of metaphors and imagery of nursing and the spiritual life. But it's not the time. I get to do a lot of looking at my life through spiritual eyes - and right now, I just need to mark this moment for what it is to me: a big change that is quietly disappearing. Wesley is just fine with his bottle of milk each evening. We still cuddle and sing and whisper and smile. We're still connected. But it's different.

Another parenting transition arrives. Time to let go, again. I hear more of this is coming. Joy!

<hr />

 "Mom, you gave me one cracker. Dad usually gives me three crackers. He tells me not to tell you."

— ISABELLA

<hr />

The Awkward Ministerial Association Meetings | January 10, 2016

I remember showing up to my first Marysville Area Pastors Association meeting at the original Living Room Coffee House location. I was nervous. I was thirty-three years old. And I was a woman. These men weren't going to know what to do with me. I stood anxiously in the middle of the room as people arrived. Sorry, as all the men arrived. I took a deep breath and wished I had stayed home to play with my kids. But instead, I smiled. Someone opened in prayer and we went through the food line. I tried to crack jokes to break the ice with the people around me. I'm pretty bad at jokes so I can never tell if that hurts or helps my first impression.

I reached the end of the line and had that junior high moment of dread. I turned around and had to pick a spot to eat. I thought junior high was in my past, but apparently when you feel insecure and out of place, the full-blown experience comes rushing back. I spotted one familiar face and rushed over to his table, while trying to look like I was meandering. Tom looked up and smiled. My spirit took a shaky breath and smiled back. He pointed to a chair at the table and I sat. Then Tom, a former district superintendent and former pastor at the church I was now serving, did one of the most gracious things ever. "Friends, this is Jenny. She's my pastor." With those two sentences, he gave me an incredible gift. In a room full of men, many who didn't believe I was called to do what I was doing, he told them a different story. Yes, she's young. Yes, she's a woman. And yes, she's called and equipped to lead people in the church.

Several guys turned to me with surprised looks on their face and we launched into the same conversation I've had for many years. "Really? You're a pastor?"

Yes. Yes I am.

For the past five years, I've continued to show up in this leadership space. Not because I always wanted to. It's exhausting to justify yourself, your call, your vocation, your worth over and over and over. I show up because they need to see me. I show up because the next young woman who comes to town and dares to enter this space might be treated as the beloved child of God she is. I show up because I've got judgmental opinions about them too. And when I keep showing up, I'm forced to wade into the churning waters of our disagreement. We may disagree mightily on important things but we are the spiritual leaders of this community and somehow, together, we make sure people get clothed, fed, and housed on cold nights. To be fair, several of these pastors have reached out to me to build a bridge on our similarities. I'm deeply thankful for the ones who risked becoming friends.

I'll never forget the day I brought Pastor Tanya and Kate along. We sat next to each other and when it came time for introductions, I stood and said, "I'm Jenny Smith, Lead Pastor at Marysville United

Methodist Church." Tanya stood and said, "I'm Tanya Spaur Pile, Associate Pastor at Marysville United Methodist Church." Kate stood and said, "I'm Kate Kilroy, Church Planter out of Marysville United Methodist Church." The room took a collective breath. Three women. In senior leadership positions. Yeah. You could almost feel their heads exploding.

Then our friend, Steve, the editor of our city newspaper, stood to introduce himself. "I'm Steve Powell, Editor of the Marysville Globe and a member of Marysville United Methodist Church." As he sat down, I breathed in an awkward and painful moment of being a woman. His presence, his position as the drummer in our worship band, and his affirmation of our leadership meant something to the other leaders in the room. Maybe they saw us differently now since Steve added his part to our story. Part of me was thankful for the validation from a guy in the room. "See, we can do this." But a bigger part of me rolled my eyes in exhaustion. We're not valid unless a man says we are.

I call BS.

 "When I'm bigger, I want to touch the sky."

— ISABELLA

Office Furniture & Power Dynamics | February 1, 2016

The first day I walked into my new office, I shivered with joy. I couldn't believe this space was mine for a season. I love decorating new spaces and creating little sanctuaries in each area of my life. This was no different. I wondered what I could put on the wall that would inspire and remind me why we're here together. I know friends would look around as they visited me in this space. What things did I want them to see?

The walls were a pale yellow and there was a large wooden desk that took up a good chunk of the room. It felt solid and intimidating. It wasn't quite my style but I found a silver lining within the first few days. When thirty-three-year-old me sat behind that desk, people took me seriously. Or at least it felt like it! Knowing this was the desk previous pastors used mattered. It was one small way to convey to folks the change in authority and leadership.

As a young woman, I was acutely aware of my relationship with power. I've breathed the air of patriarchy that shames women into quiet corners. Yes, I may be competent for the work I've been given, but that doesn't mean I don't have baggage with power and how men have used it in the world. As I sat behind that big desk, signed papers, said yes, said no, and asked questions, I also wrestled with my sense of power. *Do I have power in this situation? Am I using it wisely? I notice I'm shrinking back again. Why might that be? What do I do when someone doesn't respect my authority as their pastor and leader?*

I noticed how people responded when I made a decision they didn't like. In a corporate world, it feels like there are different rules and expectations around power than there are in the church. How do we make room for a young woman to lead with authority when we also expect her to be nice, accommodating, and respectful of all, which feels like code to never ruffle feathers?

As I got more comfortable in the role and continued to unearth what authority meant to me and how I might embody it as a leader, I felt a growing dislike for the big beautiful desk in my office. As I made important shifts on the inside, I wanted my external space to match. I set about a small office remodel as a way to match my outsides to my insides. A few of us painted the room a beautiful gray-blue color, bought a few chairs, and hung new artwork on the wall. A few new lamps meant I could finally keep the office lights off and have softer lighting. My husband built new furniture for this space that I love.

Most special of all, Aaron built me a new desk. I thanked God for the former desk as it moved on to serve another leader. I thanked God for the many decisions and conversations made around it. For the frustration, loneliness, and uncertainty seen in its presence. For the new joy stirring in a healing heart. As we moved my new desk in and I put the finishing touches on the space, I stepped back to survey the room. The desk I had asked Aaron to make was simple; a piece of wood with four legs on it. No drawers, no curves, no intimidation factor whatsoever. I wanted it to feel approachable and accessible, while also indicating it was good for a female leader to use the power given to her in responsible ways.

To others, it was just a desk.

To me, it was a daily reminder of my role. This opportunity to lead. To empower others. To make the hard and unpopular decisions. To love our team.

To others, it was just some chairs and a coffee table.

To me, it was a daily reminder of our role. The opportunity to collaborate. To partner together and wonder how to be the body of Christ in new ways. To listen deeply to peoples' stories. To empower people to step more fully into their wholeness in Christ.

I'll never forget the night Aaron and I walked into Edmonds United Methodist Church for my introduction as their new pastor. Toward the end of the meeting, a Staff Parish Relations Team member took us on a tour of the building. We walked into the office wing and I peeked through the door at the Senior Pastor's Office.

What did I see? A big wraparound desk commanding all the attention in the room.

I smiled.

I'm curious to see what I'll learn about power, authority, female leadership, and collaboration in this new adventure...

As the Day Begins

God, as I wake, tell me your good news.
Before the voices in my head warm up with their false stories,
*   tell me your true story.*

Before I greet my children and make oatmeal and toast that
*   will end up more on the floor than in a mouth, tell me*
*   about your grace.*

Before I shower, get dressed, and put on an image for the day,
*   tell me who I really am.*

Before my To-Do list gets picked back up from the day before,
*   tell me that nothing I can do today makes you love me*
*   more.*

Before I make my first mistake of the day, tell me imperfection
*   and weakness is the best place for you to work.*

Before I kiss my loved ones and prepare them for the day, tell
*   me that I'm your beloved and your love for me runs deeper*
*   than I could ever imagine.*

Before my day begins, I give you these moments, God. My
*   heart, soul, and mind are quieter now then they are all*
*   day. Tell me your true story each morning. I want my soul*
*   to memorize how your true story feels.*

Because here's the thing, God. If I don't pause to hear your
*   good news first then I start to believe the easy story.*
*   Protect, defend, control, ego, pride, fear. And the easy story*
*   isn't the true story.*

These first morning moments are yours, God. Tell me your
good news.

I'm listening.

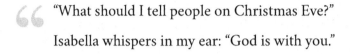

"What should I tell people on Christmas Eve?"

Isabella whispers in my ear: "God is with you."

4

THIS MIGHT BE UNSUSTAINABLE

Trust | February 6, 2016

I s it possible to be a pastor and not trust God?

Yup.

You know you've reached bedrock when you start to write the words, "God, do I dare say this out loud?" As I continue to shine a light on my autopilot and journey deep into my own life in the hopes of a new heart and way of being, I'm still uncovering patterns I didn't realize were so hard wired in there.

Sometimes it takes experiencing the resurrection before you realize the ways you were slowly dying inside.

I used to believe wholeheartedly that I trusted God. I went to seminary, made it through the ordination process, and became a pastor. Of course I trusted God.

And yes, I did trust God. But part of me did not.

Now that I'm in another season of intense growth, I look back and see a pattern of trusting myself more than I trusted God. Talk about prevenient grace. This is the grace that is gifted to us before we're aware of how God wants to move in our lives. Before, I thought I was trusting God but it was really by default. I didn't choose it very often. I tried to control life and couldn't. And after the fact, I tried to call that faith.

Ouch.

This is what anxiety does. Anxiety screams in our heads that we can't handle something. We develop all kinds of coping mechanisms to get through life. We can learn the right things to say and do to stay functional in our jobs and relationships. But when we accidentally get quiet for a moment, the truth whispers what we're terrified to admit. "This is not how you want to live."

When I look at how my trust in God has deepened this past year, it feels like I trusted what I could make happen more than I trusted God.

I'm still finding the language for how different it feels to trust God in a deeper way. Now it feels like my palms are open all the time. And that changes just about everything in my life.

It feels like I'm held.

It feels like the ground I'm standing on is stronger than the shaky mud I used to slip between my toes.

It feels like freedom.

I'm not sure I'll ever get over how surrender works. The very things we cling to for dear life can kill us. When we memorize how it feels to open our palms and let go over and over and over and over, we learn to trust the moment of surrender. We learn that on the other side of the big, scary, bottomless swirl of uncertain darkness, there is a piece of solid ground.

As we approach the season of Lent, a traditional time of giving up something and adding in a new habit or behavior, it's a perfect time to surrender. What behavior, activity or attitude needs to take a break for 40 days? Consider fasting it. We give it up for a season to make room for something new to rise. If you're feeling extra brave, go after the thing your heart tells you is the biggest distraction to your forward growth. You know what it is.

Know that God is inviting you into a resurrection this season. There is a part of you that wants to die and become something new. This is the business of God. Do you trust God enough to make the journey?

It's okay if the trust feels small. Turns out Jesus can work miracles with the little bit that we offer.

In Matthew 17:20, Jesus encourages us: "I assure you that if you have faith the size of a mustard seed, you could say to this mountain, 'Go from here to there,' and it will go. There will be nothing that you can't do."

Source | February 7, 2016

I'm reading Mandy Smith's "The Vulnerable Pastor" and I feel a load lifting from my shoulders that I was never supposed to carry.

It feels like I've been starting ministry from *what I can do* and then asking God to help as needed. When a weakness arises (fibromyalgia, anxiety, new things), I work hard to hide, avoid and push it away with better performance. I thought most of this thing was riding on me.

Apparently, it's not.

Today was a JOY to be in ministry. I shared a message I felt was helpful and important. I knew God would work through it, because that's what God does. I put my best on the table and knew it would get so much better.

I didn't hold all this tension of being liked and earning their praise. I wasn't living in fear that they would see me for who I was. I felt closer to being my actual self than I have been in a while. People might not notice from the outside -- but I know, and that's what matters.

I don't need people to like me or what I do. I'd much rather they connect with God and step into a more whole and loving life.

I don't need us to be some church or group of people that we're not. I love these people, exactly as they are. And I'm going to do all I can to give them a refuge of hope, love and transformation. And each time I meet someone with tears in their eyes after worship, I know that we're growing your kingdom, one person at a time. Incredible work, God.

Thank you, God, for changing me every day. I love this journey.

Fear | February 8, 2016

What would I do if I wasn't afraid?

Performance | February 9, 2016

I'm thinking about giving up performance for Lent. Which is scary. Am I willing to go beneath the layers of show and act to see what's underneath? What if I don't like what I find? I think about this mostly connected to ministry, but what does this look like in my marriage or parenting or relationship to others?

I've felt lately that I'm not performing in my marriage as much as I used to. I feel like I can say how I really feel and the games and manipulating are mostly over. And with parenting? I've only done it for four years so it still feels new and fresh and real. I'm pretty good at doing things with the kids that I want to do. I don't feel I'm performing for them.

But in ministry? Oh yes. Those habits run deep.

God, speak. I'm listening.

 Isabella was reading some Old Testament stories in a kids Bible one night: "Mom I'm going to be reading for a while. I'm going to get to Jesus."

I Would Love To Be Your Pastor | February 13, 2016

I got to hear someone's story yesterday. It was an honor. I was in awe of the twists and turns in her life and all the things that brought her to this moment sitting in my office. Her language for her spiritual journey left me with goose bumps for pretty much the whole hour. She wrapped up her story with a big breath and I could see the deep plea in her eyes for grace. Could this church be a place she would be welcome to figure out who she was in Christ if all the old ways weren't working anymore?

I was silent for a moment.

Then I said, "I would love to be your pastor."

A deep sigh, a couple tears and a big smile.

Friends, many of us are part of faith communities we might call progressive or open. Regardless of how we describe it, one of our values is that people can question, doubt and struggle and we don't kick them out. We welcome the questions because that's how a relationship with God works. That's how we grow!

God can handle our questions. God wants our questions. They are not a threat to faith.

A black and white framework can't handle uncertainty, wonder and struggle. It pushes them away, terrified of what might be underneath. We claim God is underneath and inside all of it. Asking the hardest, deepest, scariest questions is how we get closer to God.

I asked God to give us language for how to help people in our community understand this. And God keeps sending us people who come from a faith experience with a lot of baggage and they can't believe a place like this exists.

Thank you, God.

———

 "Mom, Wesley and I like you a little bit but we like Dad a lot."

— Isabella

———

A Spacious Community

There's room to breathe in a spacious community
There's space to bring
who you are

There's margin to explore
a new perspective

There's questions to ask
that could change everything

A spacious community
doesn't feel narrow
exclusive

41

restrictive
confining or
suffocating

A spacious community
breathes freedom into the
tight
anxious
confusing
painful
knots of our souls
In spacious community
there is
life
movement
gift
joy
sorrow
doubt
peace
love

Because a spacious community
is fully alive
Showing up with courage
Paying attention to pain
Cooperating with Love
Releasing the assumed outcome
So that Love gets a wide open playground
to skip, climb, slide and giggle
its way through us all

The Unknown | February 17, 2016

Matthew 16:25: "All who want to save their lives will lose them. But all who lose their lives because of me will find me."

What if the unknown of my new life is better than the known of my existing life?

God, where am I still doing it my way? Leading this church is tough. I feel like I'm depending on you for a lot of it. But I'm still learning to trust the spaces between things.

You give me clarity or patience and I wait for a bit. Then I want to spring into action with each new idea that passes my plate. I want to look at a great idea and say no.

Thank you for the fantastic conversation with Administrative Council last night. I so appreciate the open hearts and energy that was flowing. I give you that whole situation. Assemble a team of hearts that can best discern and listen to you as we dream and plan.

God, thank you so much for this life. For these opportunities to lead others. Work in, through and despite me today. I'm honored to be a small part of your work in the world. What a life. Yes, the unknown is far better than what I know!

 "Mom, let's make Isabella lunch, even though she's mad and didn't help with the dishwasher."

— WESLEY

My Little Bit | February 25, 2016

Matthew 6:34: "How much bread do you have?"

God, here's my little bit. Make it amazing.

Like the disciples, I look around my life, the church, our world and ask, "Where are we going to get enough food in this wilderness to satisfy such a big crowd?"

Maybe there's a better question. God, you ask us, "How much bread do you have?" The image of holding up my little bit and asking you to bless it is seared into my brain now. And what do you do with my little bit? You take it, give thanks, break it into pieces and give it to those who are hungry.

Everyone eats until they're full.

Wow. God, your power, wisdom and grace surprise me all the time. Still. All the time. Mold me, shape me, use me however you can to help people welcome your kingdom in their lives. Humble me. I'm in this for the long haul. Don't let me do this the "quick" way. No short-cuts. Let's do this the right way. I'm all in, God. Teach me how to arrange my life so you can spend me.

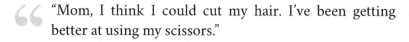 "Mom, I think I could cut my hair. I've been getting better at using my scissors."

— ISABELLA

Gratitude | March 15, 2016

My therapist asked me to list five things each night I'm grateful for.

March 15, 2016

- A family walk
- A friend to babysit
- A great Administrative Council meeting
- An incredible conversation with Stephanie
- Isabella's love of drawing cards for people

March 21, 2016

- The pouring rain
- Finishing my Easter sermon
- Taking Wesley to preschool chapel
- Confidence that fibromyalgia pain will pass
- Awareness that I've got a lot to work on in our marriage

March 24, 2016

- Wesley's first communion
- Isabella playing with Play-Doh
- Going on a drive at lunch
- A hug from Aaron
- Our kids leaving church late at night without tantrums

March 26, 2016

- Pizza
- Blue skies
- Organizing a closet
- Hard conversations
- Taking a walk outside

Don't Force It | May 12, 2016

When something changes inside our hearts and spirits, the outside world might not even notice. The change looks small or even invisible from the outside. But we know the whole world has changed on the inside.

I'm enough.

I've been in the flow. Things are working without much effort. I show up and pay attention and God is there and it goes well.

But I keep trying to prove myself. And maybe I don't have to. I can just let God do the work in and through me. Yes, I can prepare and study and pray. But I want to stop hustling and sprinting in this marathon.

As soon as my therapist mentioned flow, I said, "I thought when I got to a position like this, I would have to work *so* hard. I didn't know what it would feel like. And being in the flow feels like I'm not doing much." And then my soul opened up and I realized God's been doing the work, not me. A load was lifted from my shoulders instantly. The dam broke.

And it's time for me to open up to that. It's time to change my relationship with work.

I've had guilt about how little effort it takes to do things. I should work harder.

I've had glimpses of this wholeness and peace in my time with kids and husband but not at work. It's time.

This is incarnation. Me believing that I am enough and that Jesus does the work.

Later that afternoon, Isabella and I made paper airplanes. She threw hers hard and it wasn't going very far. I heard myself say, "it goes a lot farther when you don't force it."

Rob Bell said it well, "Grace is when we cooperate with something bigger than us. We don't fight it. I already possess that which I'm striving for. All I do is receive."

 "I don't like the quiet. My head thinks of scary things."

— Isabella

An Anger Problem | June 10, 2016

One blistering hot June afternoon, I made a stupid decision. I turned the oven on to bake something for dinner. As the room got warmer, my frustration grew. Several things that bothered me from work that day added to my frustration. I noticed my emotions rising and felt unable to stop what was about to happen.

A conversation ensued with a member in my family and I lost it. I marched over to the glass sliding door to the backyard. I opened it with indignation and stepped outside. I turned back to close the door. However, I did not simply close it. I slammed it shut.

Crack.

Uh oh.

My children stared. Aaron's mouth dropped open. I melted in embarrassment.

I had broken the glass door. And it wasn't a clean break. Hundreds of cracks rippled out from the center of the glass. I took a deep breath, collected myself and set about examining the door. We slowly opened it as the glass held in place by a protective coating. Aaron secured it with cardboard until someone could take a look at it.

I gathered the family outside and talked about what had happened.

"I felt angry. I was upset. It's okay to feel angry, right? Right. But it's not okay to slam doors. There were better ways for me to handle that. I apologize."

A few months later, I sat down to read, "The Enneagram: A Christian Perspective," by Richard Rohr and Andreas Ebert. The Enneagram is an ancient personality-type system that sheds light on our blind spots and opportunities to grow. There are nine types and many people find accurate portrayals and invitations once they determine their type. I started with the first type and proceeded to underline 90% of the chapter. Hmm.

This was the day I learned I had a problem with anger. Up until then, I rarely questioned my bursts of anger. Everyone gets angry. Once I started to read about Enneagram One's propensity toward idealism, honesty, growth, and high expectations, it felt like someone holding up a mirror to my soul. Enneagram One's wrestle with anger because they struggle to accept imperfections in themselves and others. Our brains are wired to improve, correct and reform. We get angry because the world is so imperfect. We deeply value presenting as a good person. We develop strong reaction controls so others don't know our true emotions.

That's why I could break a glass door and lack awareness that I struggle with anger. Working with the Enneagram was one of the key dominos that led me down the path of resurrection. Before that, I was busy living a polished life as a way to outrun whatever lurked beneath.

Turns out having to tell the Trustees at your church that you broke their glass door is one way to own there might be some things you need to work on.

I'm Tired | August 13, 2016

God, I'm tired. My life is too full. And I don't know how to slow it down. Help me.

Do I say no to everything for a season? I sense it's more than adjusting my calendar. My default is to do more and add more without a thought to what it will mean.

Thank you for working in and through me, especially when my soul feels like a distracted whirlwind.

I love to go through life drinking from a firehose. Create more. Promote more. Inspire more. Be intentional more. Do that new thing now.

How do I learn to pause with every new thought, idea or goal?

 Isabella: "Mom, Wesley's loving me!"

Me: "How do you know?"

Isabella: "He's looking at me!"

A Full Freezer

I want a freezer full of bread
when you promise to give me
what I need for today

I hear you
but I don't believe you

I try to buy all the bread on sale
to fill my freezer

So next week
next month

next year
I'll have what I need

As I walk down the grocery aisle
trying to grab everything
I think I need
You smile
And invite me to put the bread
Down

You gently say,
"Child,
I am all you need
You think a freezer full of bread
will be your guarantee
your promise of safety
But it won't –
it can't be

Only I can be."

I go home with one loaf of bread
to open the freezer
only to notice
it's been
unplugged

Charm | August 16, 2016

God, I need you. Show me how to be me. I want to slow down my work pace in my soul. No one else suggests I do all the things I do. It's me. I have an image in my head of what I must do to be effective. Why do I do that?

I sense that the more people "love" me, the more I work for their approval.

In "Present Over Perfect," author Shauna Niequist says it well:

> "It's easy to be liked by strangers. It's very hard to be loved and connected to the people in your home when you're always bringing them your most exhausted self and resenting the fact that the scraps you're giving them aren't cutting it. And many of us are too exhausted from the work we love to get down on the floor with our toddlers, or stay in the second hour of a difficult conversation with our spouses. It seems to me that one of the great hazards is quick love, which is actually charm. We get used to smiling, hugging, bantering, practicing good eye contact. And it's easier than true, slow, awkward, painful connection with someone who sees all the worst parts of you. Your act is easy. Being with you, deeply with, is difficult. It is better to be loved than admired. It is better to be truly known and seen and taken care of by a small tribe than adored by strangers who think they know you in a meaningful way."

God, help me think about charm vs. deep real love. I can help people feel loved right away. And it's fun. It makes me feel like I matter. But I want real love, not just charm.

Does that mean being available to fewer people? What does the balance look like?

Much of what I create is for others. I want it to stay with me longer so I can benefit from it first. I'm quick to pass it onto others.

God, I'm yours. I know you can show me.

Let Me Lead | August 31, 2016

I keep hearing you tell me, "Let me lead." It's getting louder. More firm and a bit urgent.

I'm listening.

It's almost as if I could kind of get by up to this point but now it's uncharted territory. And you're not going to let me mess this up, are you?

 Me: "Wesley, why did you draw on the wall with crayons?"

Wesley: "Because I didn't have a coloring book."

Multiplying Ministries | October 15, 2016

I checked my email on the way back from a camping trip in summer of 2016. I saw an invitation to join a cohort called Multiplying Ministries. I love leadership development. After running it by Aaron, I jumped in!

We met monthly at the Pacific Northwest United Methodist conference office for a day with Brian Zehr, a pastor and developer of leaders from the Midwest. We got coaching calls in between meetings, all with the goal that by the end of this nine-month experience, we'd have the tools and confidence to multiply our existing ministry in some way. Plus, my dad got the same invitation so I'd get to see him once a month that year!

The only downside to this commitment was that I'd have to drive to Des Moines, near SeaTac, each month. Especially in the rain. Which gives me lots of anxiety. So I bought a ticket on the shuttle from a local hotel to the airport and a colleague picked me up. We pulled up to the office, checked in, got situated and said hi to folks. Then we were off!

In the first session, we talked about things that have become part of my leadership DNA now.

People over programs.

The enemies of multiplying ministries are complexity, control, complacency & concern.

Culture is everything.

Values, Narrative, and Behavior. People are used to behaviors designed on values they used to have. When we define values for this season, we get to shape a new narrative, which can shift behavior.

The ghost mission in most churches is "how can we please everybody?"

We talked all things change management, self-leadership, building teams, vision and training leaders. My head was spinning as I boarded the shuttle bus home bound for Marysville during rush hour. I had a while to sit by the window and think. I scrolled through a few of my notes and noticed my tight throat and tears stinging the corner of my eyes.

"Jenny, what are you afraid of?"

"That I'll burn out."

Well, of course starting a cohort with these new invitations would unearth one of my core fears in life. I'm terrified of burning out. It's not that I'm afraid I could fail. Or that people won't understand. I'm okay with that. I know deepening leadership development is fun, exciting and energizing for me. It is faithful to the call of Christ. I know it's also difficult at times. But what woke up that day? My deep fear of burn out. This fear has stopped me multiple times in the past.

I'm not stupid. I've watched countless people in ministry walk away because they got burned out. It's like a secret whisper in the air between all people in ministry: *Be careful. It's coming for you too. It's not a matter of if, but when. You'll overwork. Do too much. Take on too many things. The expectations are so high. It's impossible to say no and have boundaries. Don't even try. You're always needed by someone.*

I've been listening to that secret whisper, just like everyone else. But somewhere in my journey with fibromyalgia, I learned I've done the work to have healthy boundaries so I can be sustainable for the long run. But my fear hadn't been dealt with so I still believed I would succumb to the same story of burnout so many others had walked before me.

I desperately wished for sunglasses to hide the tears spilling out of my eyes. I jotted down a few notes in my phone as I leaned into those feelings.

God, I don't want my hang ups or avoidance of burnout to keep me from the deep water you're calling me into. I'll follow if you promise to meet me there.

As I moved through the end of 2016 and into the beginning of 2017, this cohort became a container for my five-month meltdown. This was the season I woke up to how bad my anxiety had gotten and how much it shaped my life. We elected Trump during this season as our president. I didn't know how to lead through that initial season of conflict and pain among our people. Panic attacks during preaching started up again. I experienced deep anxiety almost every day and yet continued to function in ministry at a high level. This part always scares me a bit. We humans can hide so much of our fear and dysfunction behind achievement. No one could have stopped me because hardly anyone knew how bad it was, including me.

I continued attending cohort gatherings each month. I loved them! I took all the notes, asked the questions, brainstormed with colleagues and challenged myself to name what I wanted to unlearn so I could see a new way forward.

We learned about relational apprenticing, which I practiced with my friend, Lisa. Over months of learning together and supporting her, she took a deep step of trust and took over a Bible study group I had started. She was nervous and unsure. But she felt safe enough to jump! Watching her trust God and herself a little more each week was a beautiful sight.

Relational apprenticing included a little teaching that served as a powerful shift for my local church in that season. ICNU. "I see in you..." It was a simple invitation to name what we saw in people. It's so easy to let these things go unsaid. Developing a practice of being intentional about this was a game changer. As a staff team, we practiced naming gifts we saw in each other. It was a meaningful way to connect.

My other favorite use of ICNU was in large groups. Now, this was probably fairly risky and possibly stupid, but I had a feeling if I could pull it off, it would be powerful for a large group of people. In a spring leadership gathering that year, I modeled an ICNU conversation and identified several people in the room and told them what I saw in them, in front of the rest of the room. Tears sprang to eyes. The room was silent. I sensed people wanted me to call on them and not call on them at the same time!

One Sunday a year or so later, I decided to use ICNU as a sermon illustration. I walked around and chose five people in each service and shared what I saw in them. This simple act built trust and respect in our church. It deepened their relationship with me, their pastor.

We transitioned into a single board governance in that season, so it gave plenty of fertile ground to practice these concepts in our local church. A single board governance model consolidates a large committee structure into a single board that acts as Staff Parish Relations, Trustees, Finance, and Lay Leadership.

Brian introduced us to the beauty of the triangle and the square.

Preaching through this with our church proved fruitful in the months to come.

Imagine a triangle with the three sides saying, "Love God, Love Everyone, Make Disciples." These are the things we want to be a part of as a church family.

Imagine a square with the four sides saying, "Programs, Facilities, Structure & Staff." These are the things that eventually happen in any church family.

Both the triangle and square are good. However, the square often engulfs the triangle. When someone asks how it's going, people lift up the programs or groups or worship, instead of the life change happening in people's hearts. The square is important but it's transactional. The triangle is transformational. That's our true mission and purpose for existing. For leaders, it's tempting to focus more on the square because that's where we live. We can measure the square so it feels like we can control it. Life change is notoriously tricky to measure. Churches are invited to find creative ways to do the square well and remember the triangle is why we exist.

Halfway through the cohort experience, we were invited to share our hang ups that keep us from becoming more effective leaders. I named my thing about burnout. And another one found its way out of my mouth, to my surprise. *I worry about what other leaders will think of me if my church multiplies. I don't want them to think this is about my ego. That I want to be great and important at something. I hang back to not upset the apple cart.*

Shoot. Why do our secret fears jump up into the present moment when we try to keep them hidden in the dark corner? Really, God? We're going to dismantle this one too?

There's another secret whisper in the air between church leaders. *This is the way it's been done. Keep doing that. If you experiment and it goes poorly, that's okay. But if you experiment and it goes well, people will get jealous. There's this thing about competition and comparison going on. It's brutal, but silent. If you want to stay in everyone's good graces, don't dream too big. Don't step outside of what's been done.*

It's stupid, I know. But I felt it in the air. There's a decent chance it was just my fear talking. But as I shared this observation with our colleagues, they named experiences of this too. We're told to innovate but there are forces at work that aim to keep us fenced in.

Mix this in with an Enneagram One's ever-present gut check on my intentions, and it's enough to keep me in the dugout instead of swinging for the fences. I'm naturally wired to not trust my intentions. Enneagram One's want to be good and pure, yet often doubt their motives. *Sure, Jenny, you say the right things but you know what this is about. You want to be important.*

That whisper kept me from moving forward on so many interesting and creative ideas. It's embarrassing to say now. But I don't think I'm alone.

Our leader, Brian, interrupted my internal conversation with this question: "Are you doing things that require faith?" My soul took note. I so often do what I knew I could do. I find this question helpful at any moment in a Jesus follower's life. Fear will often convince us a thing is not possible. We might believe it. But our work to become more whole and grounded in the way of Jesus is an invitation to question the fears we've come to believe as true.

What if they're not?

We wrapped up the cohort in May of 2017. During this cohort, I wrestled my fear to the ground and learned incredible things about myself. I felt like a new person. Our church birthed a thirty-year vision. We prepared to add a third worship service. I felt supported and encouraged by other leaders in our conference. Our relationships with colleague deepened. We're in this together. We all win when anyone risks and takes a new step of faith. I'm deeply thankful for this cohort and how this time made space for beautiful things to unfold.

"I wish I had ten fingers. Oh wait. I do."

— ISABELLA

The Desperate Dance

There is a dance that's
never finished
A dance where you
never bow
Never hear the clapping
Never get to the end

It's a dance where you
don't even hear the music
you're dancing to
Because this dance
isn't for you

It's for others

They've watched you
dance for years
They cheer
Enjoy
Smile
burst with pride

You dance for smiles

Then one beautiful
Perfect
Healing

Holy
Day

You stop dancing for them

The desperate dance
takes one last bow

It's time to dance for joy

Control | September 30, 2016

God, sometimes I wonder if I use Sabbath as a way to control my life.
If I can get Sabbath just right, then I'll never be tired or out of control.

You Have Permission

You have permission to rest
to step off the treadmill
to not be productive
to let something slide

You have permission to feel your breath
to notice the clouds
to feel the breeze
to smell the grass

You have permission to smile
to feel sad
to be curious
to be mad

to be happy

You have permission to risk
to try something new
to let something go
to dream a new dream
to take a different path

You have permission to feel your fear
to notice the scared voice
to let it have its' moment
and then
to turn the other way
and listen to the voice that's true

You have permission to allow God
to love you in a new way
today

The True Story | October 18, 2016

We've got big changes underfoot at church, God. Keep me focused on you and listening to your Spirit. Thank you for the new names for the Vision Team. Shepherd that whole process. I trust you fully. Nudge me with what I can do to help clarify and communicate. Thank you for Anne. Help me support her well.

What does it look like for me to walk humbly with you today? I'll have a couple tough conversations. Give me a spirit of humility and curiosity. Also, the courage to draw lines, limits, and clarifications. Help me be bold in my leadership, God. These are your people and I don't want to mess around. This is life changing work. Thank you for trusting me with some of the care for this community. Help me listen to you all day long today. I want to hear the true voice of your story, not the easy story that tells me to hustle and make everything happen.

I want to move slowly with you.

Raging Gentleness

There is a raging gentleness to love
that makes no sense

How can something be
soft and strong
quiet and fierce
slow and fast
at the same time?

Love has the patience of
melting snow
and the speed of a destructive
forest fire

Love rages at injustice
Brokenness
Pain
misuse of power

Love lazily wraps its
recipients with gentleness
like a soft cozy blanket
on a cold winter day

Love is tender
Resilient

Consistent
Gracious

There is a raging gentleness to love
that makes no sense

 "Mom, I'm going to braid your hair tonight so when you wake up, you'll be beautiful."

— ISABELLA

5

THE YEAR I STOOD STILL

2017 was the year I stood still while the truth stared at me.

Therapy | January 31, 2017

Notes from a visit with my therapist:

- Let the anxiety come
- Sit with it
- The feelings will come out in their time
- No judgment of body, simply notice
- There's always freedom on the other side

I Can't Do My Job | February 12, 2017

What the hell happened? Why am I so afraid of myself? Why am I so
overwhelmed with the feelings in my body? Why do I freak out when

I get nervous with preaching? It was exhausting today trying to not have a panic attack while sharing my sermon. It takes all the joy out of it. I don't even know how you get your message across to people. It's kind of amazing. I show up, give you the little bit I have and you make it amazing. But today I was miserable while offering you what I have.

I don't like this.

I feel like a failure.

Like I can't do my job.

Why can I go from living in your flow one day to feeling utterly overwhelmed the next day?

I learned today that I've got to space out my commitments more. Too many things in one weekend is too much. If I'm going to have a disease like this than I've got to continue planning my life so you can work in and through me.

"Wait."

I sense you telling me to wait. That you are healing me. Slowly. And preparing for me something still. I'll wait as long as it takes, God.

I am yours.

Tightness | February 16, 2017

There's pain in my body and it has to come out. If it doesn't, it stays trapped. And makes me feel miserable. Not everyone is comfortable with my pain coming out. I'm sure I must confuse my husband at times. All the pain comes out in weird ways.

I'm confronting deeply ingrained patterns. It's terrifying and liberating to sense the way I've been is not how I always must be.

The tightness in my throat rises. The tears start to flow. And you heal me. Every time. And yet, this is just hard, God. I can't make people understand.

me. Every time. And yet, this is just hard, God. I can't make people understand.

I want to feel my pain. All of it. I don't want to be scared of it.

God, you are healing me. Yoga is healing me. Writing is healing me. Nature is healing me. Talking about it is healing me. Being honest about it is healing me. Crying is healing me. Reading is healing me. Hugs are healing me. Exercise is healing me.

I'm learning to feel my life and my feelings. This has been a really difficult time but I've never felt more awake to it all.

The Moment I Woke Up | February 17, 2017

I am pulling back the covers and shining a light on my fear.

This is it. I can't live like this anymore. No turning back. I have to look at the way I think and react and feel. And realize there might be great flaws in my autopilot.

This is my calling. To pull back the covers and shine the light on my brain, my feelings, my heart, my reactions, and my autopilot.

Much of my life and reactions are done on autopilot. And for me to heal and experience resurrection in this season of my life, autopilot has to go.

I am intrigued by the idea that there is a strong, confident, content space inside me that's bigger and stronger than any feeling, thought or reaction I have.

Incredible.

God, how is it possible that you've used me thus far, with all my hang-ups? It defies explanation.

Thank you.

"Anxiety is experiencing failure in advance. Tell yourself enough vivid stories about the worst possible outcome of your work and you'll soon come to believe them."

— SETH GODIN

Fear Doesn't like To Be Looked At

Fear is a bully on the playground
Perched high atop of the jungle gym
Glaring, bossing, hissing
at anyone who will listen

Most days I keep far away
from the bully
I avoid it at all costs
Sure, it keeps me confined
fenced in
half alive
but at least I don't have
to look at the bully

Until I realized the bully doesn't
just stick to the playground
Fear starts to follow me everywhere
Into relationships with people
With my body
With my mind
With my world

Then one day
the bully came for one of the things
I love the most

and I finally said

Enough

Someone told me
I could look right at the bully
with kindness
compassion
sympathy

And you know what?
I gazed at my fear with kindness
and it softened
It slinked down from the monkey bars
where it had been
terrorizing the playground

I smiled at my fear
and it sheepishly sat in the swing
next to me
Fear even started to smile itself
as it pushed its feet into the gravel
Fear started swinging back and forth
Higher
Higher

And my fear turned into joy

Comfortable | February 21, 2017

I had a wonderful appointment with my therapist today.

I felt comfortable for the first time in a long time. Like I was truly myself. A space opened up in me that was me. Not what someone else wanted or expected. It was me. It was amazing. It felt strong, content, and comfortable.

It makes me realize I haven't felt truly comfortable for a long time.

It felt like I could feel all my feelings and the space inside of me could handle it. Everything is welcome.

A small part of me usually feels frantic. Trying to define what I should be feeling and doing in each situation, instead of simply feeling how I feel and letting that be.

God, teach me how to let the frantic go. To recognize when I'm doing it.

When I have a realization and a bit of a breakthrough, it makes me think about all that came before. God, I love who I was, I love who I am, and I love who I'm becoming.

I want to feel my feelings, not other people's feelings. I've always told myself I'm an empathic and feeling person for others. But maybe my extra sensitivity to others was a way to avoid my feelings. They were so big and hard to sort out. So I went out of myself and chose to feel deeply in other people's worlds. But not my own.

I want to feel my world deeply. Bring it on, God. I'm ready.

We talked about anger, which was the thing that brought on these new thoughts. I didn't have the language to talk about my anger because I rarely let myself feel it. I've used my reaction controls for so long that I don't even know how to feel anger. And I definitely don't know how to deal with my anger.

I'll never forget sinking into my chair even further. I felt grounded in a way I haven't felt before.

My autopilot has spent years making sure that I'm feeling the right thing I'm supposed to feel and that I'm doing the right thing, by someone else's standards.

I must ask, in what ways does my autopilot keep me from receiving the grace of God? If I have already pre-determined how I feel about things without any second thoughts or grounding in reality, then how do I truly feel and receive God's grace in this moment? This disconnect is what enables me to be someone who offers grace to others but has such a hard time receiving it myself.

I continue to dismantle my autopilot. All the automatic reactions to thoughts, sensations, and feelings. All the ways I've already decided how I should feel. I question each of them now.

This space that's opening up in me is incredible. It's me. I've spent years resisting, pushing away, denying feelings that were perfectly normal to feel. And after years of doing this, those neural pathways are strong. But now I see them. And that makes all the difference.

I was sharing this with Aaron last night and had this thought: "Until you start to get healthy, you don't know how sick you were."

God, thank you for this time with my therapist. Thank you for how you continue to work through my heart, even when it's broken. Thank you for slowly healing me. I'm in this for the long haul. Guide me, lead me, I am yours.

Tears

There are tears
You could cry
That would make
You feel
Lighter

Deep Curiosity | February 23, 2017

Is this the disconnect that causes the anxiety on Sundays?

I use the language that all feelings are welcome in this space. We bring all of who we are. *But I'm not bringing all of who I am.* My anger is not allowed. It's not even recognized. This was an autopilot I set up a long time ago and it's been running my life ever since.

It already feels different to wake up and be in a weird mood and instead of trying to get in a better mood, to simply say, "I feel frustrated about...." To let the negative feeling sit there for a moment. Then it can pass, instead of me pushing it down.

I wonder if the values/narratives/behaviors framework is helpful here. I know my values. I know the most important things to me. But my narrative has been unhealthy. Which means my behaviors are unhealthy. I'm building a new narrative that aligns with my values. It can lead to new behaviors.

God, give me a deep curiosity about my inner life, my autopilot. Where does it serve me well? Where is it off base? Help me notice those moments. Help me pause when the familiar feelings of avoidance and resistance rise. They are old friends who think they're helping me navigate difficult situations but they're really not.

God, I am yours. Mold me, shape me, dismantle the parts of me that are not you.

The Biopsy | February 24, 2017

I got an ultrasound this morning and got a call from the doctor about 45 minutes later that I have a small cyst on my thyroid. They can't tell if it's benign so I'll get a biopsy.

So many emotions.

I felt them. Noticed them. I tried not to walk down the "what if" road. A cancellation opened the possibility to get the biopsy today.

I sat in the doctor's office, shaking with nerves and trying to talk to my anxiety instead of feeling knocked over by it. "Hello anxiety. You're here. I see you. You're trying to help. I need you to know there's a space inside of me that's bigger than you."

After the biopsy, the doctor mentioned as he stood at the door of the exam room, "You are brave."

I don't feel brave. I feel scared. I feel numb. I feel confused. I feel shock. I feel like a failure that I get so upset at doctor's appointments. I want a plan. I want certain outcomes. I want to be safe. I want to feel okay. I don't want to hurt or worry. Part of me feels like this is waking me up. But I don't want to wake up this way.

Today, I sit with the pain. And with you. Jesus, I need you. So badly. I don't need you to take this all away. But I need you close by. You will renew my strength. God, I am yours. Even in this, I am yours.

Not This Way

There comes a day
when something shakes you
out of your deep sleep
Your autopilot
Your everyday life

Your eyes open to your life
in a new way
You see something about yourself
you never saw before

People tell you, "you're brave"

You don't feel brave
You feel scared
numb
confused
shock

Life is upside down
You rub your eyes
and blink
and try to unsee what you saw

Too late
You're awake

I didn't want to wake up this way

My Autopilot | February 25, 2017

Today I said to Aaron, in a quiet voice, "I'm almost glad this is happening. I could have gone on another couple of months like this. Having such an uncertain couple of days has forced me up against a wall. Do I want to practice this new way of thinking? Because now is the time to do it."

I've spent so much of my life feeling scared of my thoughts, sensations, and all that comes out of me. So I quickly learned to control whatever I could. Nothing would be unpredictable. And yet, I talk a very different game with my leadership and ministry and space with my family. The difference is jarring.

I've known the way I want to go in this life. Now it's time for my autopilot to catch up.

My autopilot has not supported the wisdom I've been called to.

"I shared my glasses with a boy at the YMCA today because he wanted to be a Wesley like me."

— WESLEY

Clear | February 26, 2017

I just stared at myself in the mirror in my office for a full minute. My eyes were so clear and spacious. They've felt cloudy before. I never quite knew what was in there. I'm starting to see it.

And it's beautiful.

Teach Me | March 1, 2017

Anxiety, don't leave until you've taught me everything I need to know.

I'm Waking Up

I'm waking up.
Glistening tears, tight throat, screaming muscles.
I'm waking up.
New questions. Old worries. Decades of an autopilot that's
    simply wrong.
I'm waking up.
Even my fear is afraid.
I'm waking up.
You are brave, they say.
But this isn't how I wanted to wake up, I say.

I'm waking up.
Not on my timeline, not according to plan, with no controlled
outcome.
I'm waking up.

Waking up is kind of a mess. The glistening tears are close
friends.
Fingers type, words flow, music moves, branches sway, feet
dance, hands pray.
I'm waking up.
Jesus, I don't need you to take this all away.
But I need you close by.
I'm waking up.

Something important is happening. But I don't know what
it is.
I want to tell the story of my waking up.
But I don't know what the story is.
Still, I'm waking up.
My life is beautifully dismantled.
Pieces of the me I've always been
are lying on the floor.
I lovingly gaze at these pieces. They're beautiful.
I was doing the best I could, I say.

I'm waking up.
Freedom.

This Is Weird | March 6, 2017

I'm not in crisis mode today. Life feels quiet. I'm not used to this. My brain has been worrying about something for 34 years. But today? I feel at peace. My body is healing. I have compassion for my kind body.

I'm present to my family and loving them with compassion, not obligation. I'm walking the line between listening and acting with things at church. I'm okay with that. I'm aware when I jump into perfectionism, fear, worry, comparison, and wanting validation. I don't beat myself up for it. I move through it and it releases. I'm choosing to meditate each day because it's a daily practice, not just because I need it to function. I'm living more from my heart than I have in years, it seems.

And this all feels quite...

Weird.

My framework has changed. Most of the content hasn't changed. But what holds it has. And I must mark this. Or I fear I'll return to what I knew before. The old framework of fear and perfectionism was comfortable. My brain and heart knew the ins and outs of it well. But that framework doesn't serve me anymore.

This story must come out of me because I have to mark this season as a resurrection, otherwise it might just become a rough patch followed by a couple of new insights. Then I'll pick the old framework back up.

There's no scrambling and trying to find solid ground. I am who I am. Freedom.

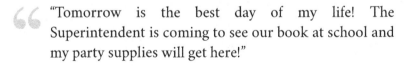 "Tomorrow is the best day of my life! The Superintendent is coming to see our book at school and my party supplies will get here!"

— ISABELLA

Imperfection | March 15, 2017

My pure joy this morning doesn't come from mastering something or proving I'm getting better. I'm not necessarily "figuring something out." My heart senses deeply that I'm content, I'm okay, I'm safe. This makes all the imperfections okay.

With all this practice of surrender, the space inside of me grows. It feels more like home, more like God. Safe. I feel myself drawn to silence. I go inside of myself when it's time to make a decision, instead of to my monkey brain chatter.

Fascinating session with my therapist yesterday. I experienced a moment where my body tried to protect my heart from caring. My tight jaw hissed, "Back off. We've got this." Then I offered compassion to the tightness. The tightness moved to my cheeks and then came out as tears. My thinking mind believes it's helping by defending and protecting my heart. May I have deep compassion for my mind. It does so much good. And may it not be scared anymore.

Unexamined Pain

Pain is neutral
Our stories force
it to take sides

Our memories
shout a story
about pain
that may not be
true
anymore

Sit with it

Let pain speak
Notice
Be curious

It will tell you
something

Once pain gets
a non-anxious
audience
a new story
can emerge

Maybe even the
pain was scared

All the Sparkles | April 3, 2017

Erin, what happens after the waking up? When the path you've walked for decades seems to beckon and shout for attention and you're stuck in the spot where the new thing isn't as shiny, it's just faithful and quiet. I need someone to hear how hard it is to keep waking up. The first time is cake compared to waking up the second, third, and fourth time. God is so patient with us.

Freedom lives in the faithful quiet path. But everything wired in me shouts for the path I know. Big fixes, dramatic moments, anxious thoughts, worry, something I can fix. Anything to avoid the quiet within.

I can't fix quiet. I can't control quiet. I can't manipulate quiet. I can't cover up my imperfections in the quiet.

I want to choose the quiet today. It's not as exciting as it first was. But

I sense it's more important than ever that I choose it.

Erin responds, "The waking up calls us to deeper things, and the deeper things are rarely as sexy as the sparkly things that float on the surface."

I press further, "But the new things should be sparkly as our reward for giving up the other sparkly things."

Erin taps out the perfect response: #allthesparkles.

The Next Layer | April 7, 2017

It feels like I broke through the first layer of autopilot and now I'm hitting the next layers. I had my initial realization of how much this affects me and now I'm realizing those neural pathways are very strong. I've been building those for decades. I don't want to waste time now being hard on myself that I haven't fixed this already.

Instead, body and heart, I have great compassion for you. For all the ways you move in this world. I'm curious about what you think is reality and what is an old pattern whose end has come.

God, guide me. My inner five-year-old wants to play. My inner twenty-year-old wants to fall in love. They don't want to be anxious anymore.

The In-Between

The in-between is quiet
Too quiet
Awkward
Uncomfortable

At first glance
the in-between
has no purpose
It's to be avoided
escaped
resisted
but something happens
in the in between

I don't have words for it yet

But it feels important
Quiet, but important
I'm used to a loud life
loud feelings
The empty quiet is weird

Jesus | April 9, 2017

I stood in my office on Sunday morning as joy and laughter filled the building before our first worship service started. The community was gathering. Friends were hugging. They were happy to be there.

And the thought hit me.

Are they coming to see me? Or are they coming to see Jesus?

My heart leapt at the truth that they're coming to see Jesus.

Yes.

Freedom.

Walking in the Fog

The air is thick and heavy
What was familiar is fuzzy
You take one step
and then another
The chill in the air
taunts you with doubt
Sure you're on the right path?
What if you're not?
What if you're confused?
What if you're scared?

You long for clarity
Wisdom
A plan

Could you trust
the answer will come
when you start walking
in the fog?

 "Isabella, I'm glad you like me again."

— WESLEY

The Sanctuary | April 25, 2017

One evening I sat in the back row of our sanctuary and watched my six-year-old daughter participate in her first liturgical dance rehearsal. Five young girls danced and spun around the room as they worked out the steps together. They laughed, danced, and laughed again. Hot tears rolled down my cheeks as I was transported back to the many dance rehearsals I participated in during high school. A group of us loved creating dances for worship or special gatherings. As the song washed over us, it was an act of worship as we imagined what the dance might look like. I loved every step of that process with those groups. It was theological work as we talked about what each step or movement signified.

I blinked my tears back and focused on my daughter. For her, this sanctuary was a place to feel comfortable. I was shocked by the next line in my brain.

The sanctuary used to be a place for you to connect to God too. Now, the sanctuary is a place to perform for others.

Uhh. Shoot. Truth.

Since the first moment I stepped foot in the Marysville sanctuary, it's been a room to prove myself. To see how many people we can get in there. To impress people. To show we were effective as a church. To have panic attacks. To feel stressed and anxious and nervous. To feel on display. A room to escape.

Watching my daughter dance reminded me a sanctuary is not supposed to feel like that.

I reached out to a therapist friend, Melinda, in our church community and she agreed to meet me in the sanctuary to do some coaching work.

One early morning, before anyone else was in the building, we sat in the front row of chairs and I shared how the panic attacks began at my last church. Emotions and memories bubbled to the surface. Pain I had kept locked away made itself known. There was a season in my last appointment where I'd felt particularly overwhelmed. I was growing in responsibility and excited by new opportunities. Which brought new challenges. My senior pastor was out of town for several weeks and I had the lead on daily operations of a large congregation. All while pregnant with a toddler at home. I, of course, wanted to do everything right, be effective, and get the job done. This is not a great mix with pregnancy exhaustion, newly diagnosed anxiety, and a sheer determination that no one could ever know how bad it was inside. Hell, I didn't even know how bad it was inside. That would come four years later.

I remembered one Sunday I had to preach through a head cold. Something snapped in my brain and I freaked out. Through the congestion, it felt like I couldn't breathe. My brain started screaming at me to get out of the room. My entire being felt grave danger. But there was no other pastor to quietly nod to while I walked out of the room. I turned to the last person on earth I wanted to ask for help. I leaned over to a staff person (we had not been getting along) and whispered, "I need to leave. I don't feel well." In the middle of the sermon. She covered for me and finished the service. I went to my office, closed the door, and sank to the floor with my head in my hands.

I felt like a failure. Especially in front of her. The little girl in me wanted to do a good job. And I wasn't yet capable of knowing everything was okay. I was doing the best I could at the time. Anxiety lies all day long about reality. I couldn't see it. I believed the fear.

I remember asking my dad to preach at the evening service that day because I was still so jittery and anxious that I couldn't pull it together. I sat on the floor sipping a cup of soup that my mom had picked up for me. God, did I feel pitiful. Shame hissed at me, "What's gotten into you? How could you let this happen? Pull it together!" But my shaking heart and body couldn't muster it. I tried to receive the grace of those who picked up what I had to put down. But I couldn't get there. This was my job and I couldn't do it.

The anxiety continued for months while preaching. I stepped up there to encourage, invite, and challenge people to follow Jesus in beautiful ways. But I spoke with one eye over my shoulder, waiting for the panic to jump up and get me.

Anxiety fiercely rose a few more times during my time with that faith community. I continued therapy here and there. I knew this pattern was not ideal, but I didn't yet see how deep it ran in my psyche and habits. I got the call to come to Marysville and professionally-speaking I was ready so we jumped at the chance. All the while, I was "managing" the anxiety well enough to function in my day to day life.

It's amazing what humans can wade through while we mask our painful truths underneath.

Back to the early morning in the Marysville sanctuary. Melinda helped me see that I had internalized a voice from four years ago that told me I would fail again. My body hard wired those feelings to that experience. So now, every time I get up to preach, my body tries to protect me from failing again.

She invited me to share the story of that past pain multiple times while doing a specific coaching exercise meant to unhook habitual responses from past events. I stood in that sanctuary and repeated new truths and my being received them as true.

I'm safe now.

I'm supported.

They believe in me.

I'm competent in this work.

I want to feel comfortable in your sanctuary, God.

Sanctuaries used to be a place I felt safe. I wanted to feel safe again.

My dearly beloved therapist friend gifted me that April morning with a new beginning. I am forever grateful.

Looking back, it made sense why this sanctuary didn't feel safe to my heart. I was still trying to prove and earn and perform. The grace of our God is that even while I was doing all that, God used words and stories spoken in that room to transform our church family. Pure grace.

In the Midst of Unknowing

Standing in the middle
between what has been
and what is to come feels
awkward
uncomfortable
painful
unsettling

I want to feel normal again
but I sense the old way
is long gone
and I'm glad

I think

I say I'm ready for the new
but I want it here now
so I can start to get used to it
so I can feel normal again

In times of deep shift
our ground moves
we feel off balance
unsure

Can you trust yourself
if the you you've always been
is new?

Joy | April 12, 2017

God, you've given me something to say.

And I want to say it with joy, not fear.

Who Will Stop You?

Only you know the depth
the pain
the reality
of the unhealthy patterns
in your life

Others may think they know
They can nod and care
and support and love

But they don't know

You've developed a lifetime
of skills to cope
to numb
to forget

You're so brilliant
that some days even you
forget how much it hurts

And yet
your ways of being
are so solid
consistent

automatic
unconscious
that they seem
unquestionable

They are not

Question them
Wonder
Be curious

Could love soften even that?
What if I changed?
What if I stopped holding that?
What if I let go of control?

Then even better questions arise

How might my life change?
What would it feel like to be free?
In numbing my pain,
have I also numbed my joy?
What could I do in life
if this healed?

Then comes the choice
that's yours alone to make
No one gets to make it for you

Who will stop you?

You maintain our death grip on control
and secretly hope someone will stop you
but they won't be able to
because it's your choice.

There's no magic time
to begin the work
of becoming more yourself
It won't feel great at first
It's painful to look at pain

But you won't die
I promise

Well, part of you might die

But I suspect you've been ready for that
for a long
long
long
time

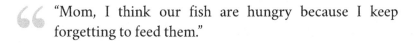

"Mom, I think our fish are hungry because I keep forgetting to feed them."

— ISABELLA

Your Five-Year-Old You

There's a voice deep inside you
that you likely haven't listened to
in a long long time

A voice that's scared
Uncomfortable
Angry

Confused

You may have been taught to
push that voice away
as you grew up

You had a life to live
A new self to create
and put on
for the world

A self where you were in control
Competent
Put together

The longer you live that life
the deeper the voice
gets buried

But the beauty of this voice
is that while it's buried beneath
insecurity
pain
Isolation
fear and
indifference,
it's ready to speak to you
whenever you're ready to listen

The voice is you
Your inner child
Five or six years old

And they've got something to say
when you slow down and listen

They may tell you about a need they had
that didn't get met

They may whisper to you a fear you had then
that's still shaping you now

They may look at you through tears
and tell you how hard they were trying
but they didn't know what to do

Because you're not five or six anymore
You know how to listen now
You feel their pain

Sit with them on a bench while they share

You're stronger now
It hurts
a lot
but you know you can do this

And over time
Days
Months
Years
of visiting this part of yourself
They teach you what you need
to do now
to be whole
at peace
free

If you're willing to do the work
To give yourself what you need now
One day you'll check in with your inner child

and they will gratefully say,
"Thank you."
"Thank you for helping me understand."

Wholeness
Integration
Freedom.

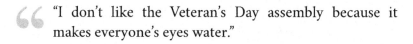

"I don't like the Veteran's Day assembly because it makes everyone's eyes water."

— ISABELLA

6

A WAY IN

The Easter Sermon Where I Told My Truth | April 17, 2017

D o you remember being five years old? I remember taking a nap in kindergarten, playing at the sand and water table, and some boy pulling my ponytail on the playground. I'm having the time of my life watching my five-year-old navigate her world. She recently said, "I don't like when the boys be loud. They're loud all over the place." One night at dinner she asked, "Can we plant mashed potatoes?"

We all have a five-year-old inside of us that's holding a brightly colored balloon. We're fascinated by it. It bounces along, goes where we go, we have no other goal than watching what this balloon does. Pure joy and curiosity. Wide awake and bright-eyed. That five-year-old is in you. Some of you know this and you're in touch with this five-year-old. They come out to play many days.

But many of us don't know this five-year-old anymore. We took their balloon away a long time ago. Popped a hole in it and watched the air rush out with a force that took part of our soul with it. Or maybe we let go of something important to us and it simply drifted away.

Someone hurt us so we started to armor up. We figured out how to protect ourselves from getting hurt again. The five-year-old packed up their toys and faded into the background.

Now we walk around as adults seeing the balloons of others and wondering why we can't just be like them. Everyone else looks like they've got it together. We hide our half-deflated balloon inside, trying to protect the air we've got left. Just trying to get through life.

But here's the thing. The One who created you wants you to know your five-year-old self. To know joy, curiosity, childlike faith. God wants you to play, to hold your balloon full of glorious air with delight.

Today, I want to tell you about a resurrection. About new life in the midst of fear. A story about getting a new balloon. Yes, the Son of God walked to the cross, was crucified, he died and was buried. And on the third day, he rose from the dead. He woke up and death died. I could tell you about what Jesus did back then. But this morning, I'm going to tell you what Jesus is doing today.

Like in the last four months.

In me.

I've struggled with high functioning anxiety and panic attacks for all of my adult life. Somewhere along the way, I believed the lie that if I could just be perfect, life would be okay. I would be safe. I wouldn't get hurt or feel discomfort. Or feel out of control.

These patterns became deep ruts that guided my life. There was no getting out of them. They were facts, it seemed. The fear of imperfection, failure, being out of control was always close by. So much so that I learned to construct a life around them.

The absolute grace in this life is that I created a life I love, while being afraid. A spouse, our children, this calling to be a pastor. This is the life I want. I found I could walk with God deeply even while dragging a deflated balloon behind me. And the thing about perfectionism is that lots of energy went toward denying the balloon was even deflated. It still amazes me that we can surrender parts of our lives to the resurrection power of Jesus Christ, and other parts of our lives continue in dysfunction. It's almost like grace is real. Jesus comes to us in our mess, not our perfection.

I go on to sense a call into ministry, go to college, get married, go to seminary and graduate. All these changes brought my anxiety to the surface. I was growing up, gaining more responsibility, and my inner perfection drive could hardly keep up. Anxiety was trying to get my attention, to tell me to look inside and face the things I was afraid of. But I didn't listen. Like Dory says, "Just keep swimming, just keep swimming."

The thing about high functioning anxiety is that no one knows it's happening. I still function. Fairly well on the outside. But I wasn't at peace inside. My insides did not match my outsides.

Several years ago, I started to have panic attacks while preaching. But no one knew. I could stand up with a smile on my face and share a meaningful message of grace and hope, and inside, my body was screaming. "Get out of here, you're going to fail, you're not in control, just get out that door." I would be terrified of those happening. My heart was trying to talk to me: "Wake up. Stop sleeping. Look inside your life. Let me speak."

That sense of fear and dread was ironic as I preached on Sunday mornings that God offered us joy and peace in this life. Sometimes, I think I preached mostly to myself. Others just got to listen in. I so desperately wanted the good news of Jesus to be true. Part of me knew that it was. Almost as if my balloon was half-filled with air from God and half-filled with stale air from my fear.

Fast forward to this past fall. We've all been a bit shell shocked as our country figures out how to navigate these confusing times. Needless to say, I sensed the anxiety in our country, in my friends, family, and our church and felt it deeply. I wondered where God was calling me to respond and lead. I found myself holding a couple of things in tension. Where's our call to be prophetic, to lift up the Gospel, of a man who was crucified because he challenged and subverted the political system of his time? Where's our call to be a safe place for everyone, where we can be in relationships, even though we see things from different perspectives? Then as the inauguration happened and the women marched and the world braced itself for what might happen next, my anxiety was speaking out, loud and clear. The panic attacks while preaching started again. Here, in this room, several months ago.

A couple of days after one of those, during my annual physical, my doctor felt something on my thyroid and asked me to get an ultrasound. As I drove home from that appointment, she called with the results and said she wanted to do a biopsy. "To be prudent, to be sure it was nothing." My heart sank. Seriously? With everything I'm trying to navigate, now this? I got a biopsy that Friday afternoon and entered into the waiting.

And I knew right away that this was a moment I needed to pay attention to. I could continue in this ridiculous dance of acting like I was fine when I wasn't fine. Or I could do the thing I knew God was inviting me to.

To wake up, again. To a new area in my life where Jesus was not Lord. To journey into the places in me that I've avoided, out of pure fear. To shine a light on my autopilot and habits that were sucking the life out of me. To remember resurrection means God does God's best work in places that appear dead and lifeless.

So I did it. And the voice that called on Monday afternoon and said, "It's benign," was nice. But the gift of being forced up against the wall and seeing my life with new eyes, that was gold. So here's what resurrection looks like to me this year.

Resurrection is showing up to therapy every week.

Resurrection is downloading a meditation and prayer app and

learning how to sit still and let the inner drama of my mind start to settle down. This can feel terrifying at first. It was the exact space I'd avoided for years. But after three months straight of practicing, I'm now comfortable with the silence. It's teaching me everything I need to know. God is there. My heart is there. My soul can breathe more deeply because it has space. Everything falls away that's not important. Life has gotten lighter, simpler, more joyful.

Resurrection is kind of a mess. It doesn't happen on our timeline and has no controlled outcome. For me, it means tears, writing, walking, listening, questioning, and sharing.

Resurrection is seeing the voices of shame for what they are. Lies that we picked up along the way and believed deep down in our soul. Those voices don't get to tell us who we are. Only the One who created us gets to do that. The problem is we don't usually get quiet enough to listen.

Resurrection is asking new questions in spaces where you were sure the old assumptions were true.

Resurrection watches the pieces of your life become beautifully dismantled. Pieces of the you you've always been are lying on the floor and it's simply beautiful. It takes your breath away when you realize you don't need those pieces anymore.

Resurrection is meditating and praying one quiet afternoon in a silent home. And bringing to mind an image of my five-year-old self and asking if there's anything she wants to say. I look around, thinking this is kind of weird. But I stay quiet anyways. I feel an image of my five-year-old self pulling on my shirt saying over and over...

I just want you to be safe.

I just want you to be safe.

I just want you to be safe.

I said to her, "I am safe." Tears flowed. More than I'd cried in years. I comforted the five-year-old in me, who hadn't gotten to grow up yet, because she was so afraid. I sank deeper into my life that afternoon.

Resurrection is realizing I can tell my church that all of who we are is welcome here, God can handle it. And maybe that even means me.

Resurrection sees the despair in skimming the surface of our existence. The best parts of us are below the surface. Way below the surface. Resurrection calls us to those places.

And in those places, we find freedom and joy. What if our freedom lives inside our fear?

Friends, I simply had no idea how much the patterns of fear had shaped my life. They set up camp and I learned how to circle them. I didn't know I could welcome them in and ask some questions and that they had something to teach me.

People in the Jesus story knew fear. The guards were terrified. The angel tells them there's nothing to fear. The disciples are afraid but they listen anyway. Jesus tells them not to be afraid.

Why is fear such a theme in resurrection? A new life, a new shiny, bouncy, joyful balloon is given to us, and we're terrified. Are we scared of joy? It can feel out of control. Are we scared of becoming new? Of leaving the known of our fear to enter the unknown of what Jesus is offering? Yeah, probably.

Think for a moment about the places in you or in this world that you've avoided. The rooms you locked a long time ago and put up yellow caution tape and a "No Trespassing" sign.

Jesus wants you to go into those rooms. Because He's already there. Waiting for you to open the door.

What might you find? I don't know. But it'll be okay. Because Jesus walked to the cross, was laid in a tomb, and rose again, I know Christ is alive. In you. In me. In the people who drive us up the walls. Christ is holding out a simple, joyful balloon full of new, clean, fresh air. A new way to breathe. A new way to wake up.

And that fear? It's still with me. And the thing you're trying to outrun? It'll stay with you for a while. But we don't have to be afraid of it anymore. I'm ready to call it out when I see it and choose a different path.

This Jesus stuff works, friends. It sounds cheesy but I knew this Easter, if I was going to tell you about a resurrection, I was going to have to tell you about mine. New life is beautiful. It's overwhelming. It's work. But it's real. And after looking everywhere for it, even becoming a pastor, I found it again in Jesus. Who would have thought?

My waking up has been about integration. About fitting the different parts of my life together in one new story. Recently, my husband drew a powerful image and framed it for me. It's me holding the hand of my five-year-old self on one side and the hand of my 20-year-old self on the other side.

My five-year-old self is learning the world isn't such a scary place. My 20-year-old self is learning it's okay to trust, to fall in love again, and to be vulnerable. What a gift to look at this each day!

Friends, never underestimate the power of community on these journeys we make. You are not alone. If you're looking for a community of friends, we'd love to be your community. We're not perfect, but we show up.

Romans 6:4: "Therefore, we were buried together with him through baptism into his death, so that just as Christ was raised from the dead through the glory of the Father, we too can walk in newness of life."

Happy Easter, my friends. Jesus is alive. May that be good news to your heart this day. Amen.

 Me: "Wesley, did you have a good Easter today?"

Wesley: "No, you made me wear this dumb shirt."

New Clothes | June 2, 2017

My journey feels like I've been wearing 100 layers of clothing. I was uncomfortable and hot and agitated and anxious with all those clothes on for years.

Then I decided it was finally time to get curious about why I was wearing so many clothes.

One by one, I picked up a shirt and tried to see if that one was serving me anymore. Once I realized it was an old way of thinking or acting or believing, I let it go. Some pieces of clothing were easy to discard. Others I wrestled with for days or months. Still others I took off but then kept putting them back on without realizing it.

Once in awhile I would take stock of the closet I was wearing, and realize a couple layers of clothing disappeared and I didn't even know when or how. But I was deeply thankful.

Now I don't know how many layers of clothing I have left until I get to who I am. But I know that I'm getting closer. That brings unspeakable and indescribable joy.

There is a trail of old worn out clothes behind me.

Some of the clothes don't serve me well but I suspect they'll always be in my closet. And that's okay. I see them, I've inspected them thoroughly, turned them over in my hands. I know every thread in those clothes. They don't surprise or scare me anymore.

Some clothes are so worn and tattered and filled with holes but I can't bear to part with them yet. They're comfortable and known. I used to think they were my favorites. But I slowly am realizing it's time for the favorites to go. They're keeping me from receiving the new clothes God has for me.

Finding the Right Clothes

When I stumble into a new season
full of change, picking up, letting go
of plans, dreams and identities
Nothing fits at first

It's like shopping for a swimsuit
in fluorescent department store light
No one is happy
There are tears
eye rolls
frustration
But ready or not
the new identity is here
and it never fits quite right
at first

It feels awkward
Uncomfortable
Maybe even sad

I want my old clothes back
They fit so well

But someone took them away
like that donation bag
that sits in my trunk
for months

I'm left to stand in front of the mirror
Naked
Vulnerable
Scared

I try on everyone else's clothes
thinking their life will fit my new one
but they don't

Their clothes look great on them
but they're not my clothes

Then one day, after time has passed
and I slowly understand and accept
my new identity, dream or reality
I finally find a shirt that fits perfectly
It's like it was made for me

Finally slipping into an identity
that was made for me
makes the dressing room journey
worth it

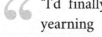 "I'd finally come to understand what it had been: a yearning for a way out, when actually what I had wanted to find was a way in."

— CHERYL STRAYED

Stay Put | June 20, 2017

Sasha Tozzi said on Instagram today: I got patient and stood still while the truth stared at me.

Yes. This has been my life these last five months. I've gotten quiet and still in a deeper way than before. And it feels like the truth is staring at me. I'm deciding if I'm going to run again or stay put. The truth is staring at me, daring me to stay. And most days, I stay put. I'm listening.

Sasha said in her caption: It's been messy and uncomfortable while immersed in it, it always is -- the breaking through, the birthing of yet another self.

The truth sits there so quietly. It's not demanding or loud. It waits to be seen. Then it starts to whisper. And that whisper changes everything I thought I knew about myself, the people I love the most, and the work I'm called to.

 Me: "I have the hiccups. What can I do to get rid of them?"

Isabella: "I can scare you."

Me: "Go for it."

Isabella: (Without skipping a beat) "Mom, I can't find your phone!"

A Milestone | June 24, 2017

I'll never forget the day Isabella finished her summer session of preschool. The last one before she started kindergarten. We snapped a picture to quietly mark a milestone. For two years, Isabella went to preschool at our church. Aaron and I worked there too. Wesley spent time in the nursery with a dear friend of ours and her daughter. It was the last day we'd all be there together in this season.

I loved this time in our lives. I knew it was a gift the whole time. I knew it would end. She would go off to kindergarten and we'd be apart. I breathed deeply of gratitude when I got to pick her up from preschool. We'd walk down the hall to the nursery and she'd run in to find her little brother. We'd talk in the hallway with other parents while the kids ran around.

I was navigating new realities in my professional life that could overwhelm me at times. Knowing my children were right around the corner was a great comfort. I scheduled meetings around the school schedule so I could be waiting outside their door as they ran out to greet me.

I knew I'd never get this season back. I'm thankful to this church for the gift they gave me. We're in grief as this preschool closes its door this year. As I wander the empty halls, peering into each room and remembering my three and four-year-old's smiling and playing, my heart swells with gratitude. This is a gift I'll treasure for the rest of my life. I got to be both pastor and mom in the same building for two years when it mattered the most. Thank you, Stable Beginning Preschool. I'm forever grateful.

 "You know the song, 'Life is a Highway?' Are we on that highway?"

— WESLEY

I Wish I Never Woke Up

Some days I wish I never woke up
That I never saw my actual life
hiding under what I thought was my life

Some days I wish my pain was still asleep
Still oblivious
Still invisible

Life felt easier when I was unaware
Unencumbered by my actual reality
This new life takes so much work
The questioning
The curiosity
The sitting-with
The witnessing-to
The willingness to look directly into pain
that I so expertly kept tucked away
behind nice smiles
nice conversations
nice plans

It feels like my old life was easy
I thought everything was fine
but only because I was asleep to it

Sleeping soundly through pain
isn't a beautiful way to live

Living half alive
isn't a great way to live

Still
Some days I wish I never woke up

Hardwired | June 26, 2017

When you move from doing things because you're *supposed* to, to doing things because you *want* to, it affects every level of your life.

I've spent my life looking for clues everywhere to make sure I'm doing the right thing. This is what perfectionists do.

How different to move through life listening to a different voice.

I lean on food to save me and fix situations and give me solid ground. It's a type of aggression towards food. I need it to be something for me.

No wonder I don't have a nourishing relationship with food. I depend on it for something it was never intended to be.

Can I look deep into the eyes of another person with true compassion if I am unable to look into my own heart and soul to see what's going on? Our connections with other people change when we have done the work inside of ourselves.

When I haven't had compassion for my husband, how often has it been because I haven't had compassion for myself? Compassion for my kids somehow circumvents that whole process.

If I secretly am hard on myself and withhold compassion from myself, then I would naturally withhold compassion from other adults. "If I don't get it, you don't get to have it either." It's hardwired deep in there.

Control | June 27, 2017

While swimming and floating on my back at the YMCA this afternoon, I prayed, "God, I trust you. But..."

The "but" is what causes my suffering. It's me pretending to let go but not really doing it. It's me making a good show of following God but not trusting the God who made me.

It's all about control.

Pruning | July 10, 2017

God, you are pruning me.

Cutting off good things so better things can come.

I'm good at empowering people and it's working but it doesn't feel like "effective work" to me yet. Other people are doing it. So I keep generating activity to show I'm doing something. But these beloved people are being empowered. I'm making disciples. *That* is my work.

Help me see that, God.

I'm good at creating momentum. But now comes the phase where we build something that can last. I haven't gotten to do this part much before. It's unknown. I'm nervous. How do I navigate this? I don't want to mess it up.

I want to work differently.

I see the threads coming together. I want to make disciples more than I want to grow a church in numbers. What are we measuring? Where is our time spent?

I'm Your Home

God, you tell me I'm a temple
A home
A sanctuary

Are you comfortable here?

I hope you feel welcome
That you can be yourself
Or is it like visiting relatives
you never talk to?

A little awkward
Uncomfortable
Where you turn on the charm
but it doesn't feel true

You live in me
Do you have room to breathe?
Can you be yourself?

Better yet,
I hope you don't have to work
extra hard to do your work
through me

I know you're willing and able
but I long to be a welcome home
for your work in this world

I am yours.

Focus | July 11, 2017

I am rewarded for my activity. It's proof that I'm doing something. I want to focus more on what *you are doing* instead of what *I'm doing.*

I got by the first two years here with random ideas and energy all over the place. It's time to focus.

What could you do through me if I could focus?

Meditation Workshop | July 29, 2017

As my 35th birthday approached, I wondered if there was something I could do to mark this season of rapid change inside of myself. I decided to put together a meditation workshop! We spread the word, I put together an outline for the morning and we waited to see who might show up.

That morning, I walked into the sanctuary to have a chat with Jesus and I just laughed at him. Me?!? Leading a meditation workshop? This is ridiculous. I whispered to Jesus through tears, "You're doing everything today. I'm just showing up and paying attention."

The workshop was amazing. It felt like I had been doing these for years. It was easy and relaxing. It felt great to meditate with other people.

Thank you for sending the people and for taking me on this journey. I can't believe this morning happened. I'm so thankful.

In the following years, we walked 120 people or so through some version of a meditation workshop. I still can't believe I got to participate in something like that. God is good.

Twisted Hearts

There are days
Months

Years
where my heart is twisted

Contorted
Defensive
Stubborn

I put on armor
every morning
to protect myself

My twisted heart
is off limits
The open sign
got unplugged
The caution tape
keeps people away

Some days a twisted heart
feels righteous
comfortable
predictable
But really
If I gently put down the armor
plug the sign in
peel back the tape
my twisted heart
is
afraid

Can it trust?
Can it love?
Can it risk?

Each twisted heart

must make the journey
itself

Ask new questions
Challenge assumptions
Forgive
Feel
Held
The originator of love
Grace
Peace and
Wisdom
hopes your heart
will make the trip

The Waiting | August 31, 2017

Here again I stand. In the middle. In the waiting. Between a biopsy and a phone call. A day and a half this time. My spirit is settled. Grounded. Trusting in the unknown space to come. Whether it's a checkup in six months or a round of tests next week, I am here. In this moment. Baking birthday cupcakes with my daughter for our son who turns three tomorrow.

This is what we do, isn't it? No amount of mental gymnastics gives me a clear next step. Getting my body twisted up in knots only hurts me, it doesn't change an outcome.

Today I make an intentional choice to keep returning to this moment. It's the only thing I have a say in right now. And today, I choose that. On purpose. Not as a way to avoid what's coming next. But as a way to say thank you, God. I know you're already present in whatever is next. Patiently waiting for me.

I hear you whispering, "it'll be okay."

Arguing with Grace

"Yes, son, you can have an extra piece of candy."
"But Mooooom! He already had one today!"
"Child, this is grace.
Don't argue with grace.
Just receive it."

Do you argue with grace?

Maybe you create a long list of reasons why
you don't get the gift today
or why you didn't deserve it last year
or why that thing you did way back
has removed you from the list of grace

We're pros at arguing with grace
when other people are involved

We create a long list of reasons why
that person
and that person
and that person
should not receive grace
They said that
or do that
or believe that
or didn't do that

We argue with grace
We play traffic cop
We say yes to that person
and no to that other person

Meanwhile

Love stands at the head of the
longest table you've ever seen
and softly smiles
with arms outstretched
"Welcome, my children.
There's enough grace for all of you."

Even them.
Even you.

What if we didn't argue with grace?
What if we noticed our resistance
Smiled gently at our pride and hesitation
and chose to open our hands wide
to grace meant just for today?

What if we chose not to live on
grace from last year or last month
but shouted a massive yes
to grace for today.

Our God doesn't mess with
old worn out and tired grace
from a season long past

Our God offers
grace
A second chance
A 42nd chance
Forgiveness
A new beginning

Every

JENNY SMITH

Single
Day

Stop arguing with grace
and open your hands wide
to receive

 "Mom, when God made you, God said you were so darn good!"

— WESLEY

7
_____

WHAT IF?

Our Tree | August 17, 2017

One summer afternoon, I left the church to meet a parishioner for coffee. Instead of driving out the front parking lot, I felt a nudge to go through the back parking lot. Something drew my attention to one of my favorite trees on the back of our property. It's one of those times of the year where the sun shines through the light green leaves and it's gorgeous.

I stepped out of the car and walked over to this tree. I gazed at the leaves with absolutely no agenda.

I then had a very strong sense that this specific tree represented our ministry. My job was to hold on to the trunk. To stay connected to God as much as I could. An intense feeling came over my body as I stared at the tree. It felt like I couldn't look away even if I tried.

Then my gaze was drawn slowly up the tree and I saw it as if for the first time. Countless branches and fluttering leaves in every direction. My breath caught. The leaves represented people. I felt a strong voice inside me say, "Just hold onto me. There will be people whose names and stories you never know. Because you hold onto me, they'll be connected to me."

I continued to gaze upward as tears rolled down my cheeks. The leaves fluttered everywhere! And wow, did they look beautiful. The sun sparkled as the breeze danced. That tree came to life before my eyes.

Those leaves were connected to a branch that was connected to another branch that was connected to the trunk.

That was enough.

I felt my heart whisper to God, "I will gaze at you forever. I am yours. You are mine. I want to be fully surrendered to whatever you want to do through me."

I got in my car to head to my appointment, shaking my head and trying to make sense of what I'd just experienced. People have made fun of me before for trying to read into everything. "Jenny, not every-thing is something." But I'm wired this way. I see metaphors and examples of God's love everywhere I look. Sometimes I wish I could turn this off because yes, I imagine it's exhausting to the people around me at times. But I enjoy seeing the connections.

But a part of me shook my head at this one. *Come on, Jenny. It's just a tree. Who do you think you are? People and stories you'll never know? Right. A little too big for your britches there, dear.*

Shame jumped in for the party in my head and I tried to forget the moment.

But I couldn't.

In the months to come, our staff, the leadership team, and then our entire church spent time around that tree. We reflected on what I originally experienced, what it might mean for our sense of God's call and how we felt about it.

I'm still not sure what happened that August afternoon under that tree. Was it my wishful thinking that one day I would preach and encourage countless people to love God? As an Enneagram One, I'm hypersensitive to my motives and frequently discount my intentions. Yes, it's ironic that I second guess my desire to help people love God. I worry that I'm in it so people would know me, more than they follow Jesus. Over the years, I've worried about this so much, that it's kept me from taking steps forward that I felt called to.

Fear and shame are real. And insidious.

That message from the tree stayed with me for several years. It continued to inspire us forward. We felt compelled to make creative room for people and stories that we didn't yet know. The 30-year-vision was born out of that moment with the tree. Helping our church grieve the growth in our community was born out of that moment with the tree. The themes of pruning, trimming, and abiding in John 15 grounded us for several years as a church family.

Thank you, glorious tree, for being a physical place where I connected with God. Thank you for your inspiration, no matter the season. I was just as moved by your barrenness and brittle branches in the winter as I was by the early buds in spring. Thank you for letting me sit against your trunk as leaves fell in the fall. Thank you for the tears I shed in a quiet moment, when no one was looking. Thank you for being my burning bush, a place I encountered God and couldn't look away. Thank you for helping me see something about what it means to be a church family together.

Thank you for being holy ground.

A Wild Vision: 10 in 30 | 2017-2020

I don't want to write this story. Well, I do. But I'm having the hardest time putting this part of our journey into language. I wonder if it's because we're not done with this one yet. I wonder if this vision is still becoming, My attempt at wrapping it in language feels futile. But I'll try.

As I emerged from the fog of fear that hung over my life for years, I felt a growing invitation to dream a little beyond what I'd imagined before. As with most things, it unfolded slowly as we took one step at a time.

August 24, 2017

That moment with the tree on the church property was a big shift. This strong invitation to cling to God, to make sure our leaders do and "there will be people connected to God whose stories and names we never know" is unsettling and somehow, deeply compelling. I shared it with a few people and continue to feel curious.

October 15, 2017

I'm trying so hard to figure out a vision. Which means there isn't a lot of prayer anymore. I'm up in my head, trying to concoct a vision and plan that satisfies whatever was rumbling inside.

November 21, 2017

There are other ways to be the church and I am feeling invited to make space for that. Different models swirled around me as my heart sank a little deeper in listening.

December 5, 2017

When am I holding onto an old word and can't receive the new one? As our charge conference prepared to meet, we invited our church to pray a prayer together for the rest of Advent: God, we are yours. What do you want to do through us? I confess that I asked our church to pray as a last-ditch effort. This could have been the first thing we did. But no, it took a while for me to get outside of myself and realize the point of this process was to discern together.

About a week after we invited the church to pray, I realized they were doing it and I needed to join them in that process! As soon as I joined them in prayer, things started to simmer underneath me.

December 10, 2017

Something is shifting, God. I sense it in my spirit. I'm sad. It's not a dramatic sadness. It's quiet. Resolute. Unsurprised. Expectant. I knew this was coming.

Leading a larger faith community is asking new things of me. I'm learning and stretching and seeing the fruit already of leading differently. And there's grief. The old way made sense and it fit me like a glove. This new way feels unsettling, awkward, fitful, unsure. And yet, I already sense you calling me forward into it.

There's a grief in following you that comes after the excitement and before the thrill of the new. There's a quiet space in the middle that's...sad.

There's a saying goodbye to the familiar that's hard.

God, keep extending your hand to me on the new trail. I'll follow. Stay close. I'm letting go of a lot. I need you.

December 13, 2017

Part of me wants you to birth your vision in our community and not through me. Then I'm off the hook for hearing some dream that only you can do. My faith doesn't feel big enough. I'm nervous to put my neck out there and say something that I can't achieve.

Either way, I'll keep showing up and paying attention. I release the outcome of how your vision will birth through us. And when and how. I will listen deeply to the random thoughts in my soul. God, do your thing. We're ready.

December 15, 2017

I feel like you're preparing me still for what's next. The fear rises and tries to distract me. I'm starting to get a more clear image in my mind of what's possible with you. It's always been fuzzy. I see you opening doors so clearly. And I'm overwhelmed with tears. I don't know exactly why. I sense that you're stripping away the parts of me I don't need anymore. With each tear that rolls down my warm cheek, you gently remove the old ways of thinking and fighting and clinging. God, you're so incredibly kind and gentle as I let go. You don't take it. You receive it. You wait for me to release it and give it to you.

God, I give you my fear. Give me a spirit of courage and boldness.

May these tears soften the ground of the new thing you want to grow through me.

I release all these tired voices:

Who do you think you are?

You're not special.

What will your colleagues think?

What if it's the wrong vision?

What if my church doesn't want to grow?

It's as if the fear cycles around me like a silent tornado. I'm ready to step through the spinning wall because it simply isn't true.

God, you are calling us to support multiple faith communities coming into existence.

December 17, 2017

Having a front-row seat to your creativity and timing is fascinating. I've been praying for what feels like forever for a vision for this church. I see now that clues and hints were sprinkled throughout but only after I released the whole process to the church, could I start to see with clarity.

We invited the entire church to pray, "God we are yours. What do you want to do through us?" And now it feels like the camera lens focused in.

It feels like we released the outcomes and preferences we have about what we thought you might do. This is not anything I thought I would be a part of. I haven't liked multi-site in a long time. I didn't see how it could fit us and our leadership.

Last night at the Christmas Concert, I felt moved by the image of Mary holding Jesus. She trusted you without knowing what might unfold. She didn't know what would happen to your son and she still said yes.

God, I want to be like Mary. I want to help our church birth new expressions of faith. I don't need to know the outcomes. I trust you with everything.

I have to write it again because it gives me chills every time I say it aloud.

What if Marysville United Methodist Church birthed ten new expressions of church in the next thirty years?

What if we continued to invite our current community to be deeply committed followers of Jesus Christ while allowing God to do something significant through us?

Until recently, I've had baggage around multi-site. I've seen the downsides of it, from the inside. God is softening my resistance. I used to think multi-site was something we did. It sounded like so much work. Especially in a new context when we have plenty of work to do in our current context. Now, I sense it's a vision we get to allow to happen through us. The source of energy comes from a different place. It comes from conference-supported planters with great training and resources committed to listening deeply to what God is already doing in our area and responding. We get to cheer on the ministry while continuing to grow a beloved community at our current location.

This idea of multi-site is not new for Marysville United Methodist Church. It's been talked about multiple times in recent years. This is a next step in exploring this possibility in this season.

This is cooperating with God and releasing what God wants to do in and through us.

By 2050, we see ten new faith communities thriving in North Snohomish County. They are vibrant and alive. Each community has a deep sense of grace and love for all people. It looks different in each community. Some are clergy-led. Some are lay-led. Some are deeply connected in relationship with Marysville United Methodist Church. Some are chartered as new churches out on their own. They are all encouraged and loved by the people of Marysville United Methodist Church. The leaders of all ten faith communities are collaborative, self-aware, intentional, and grounded. They value an intentional rhythm of work and Sabbath rest. The leaders have teams full of people who are becoming whole in Christ while loving the people right in front of them. Every single person in these ten faith communities are seeking to follow Jesus by showing up, paying attention, cooperating with God and releasing the outcome. The kingdom of God is alive and growing in 2050!

January 7, 2018

There's a difference between powering through a tough situation and receiving. This weekend I'm anxious and jittery around the Vision Team meeting. Trouble sleeping two nights in a row. The old me would have powered through. Now I know to sit back, listen, and receive.

God, I'm sitting in my van in the dark at 7:20 am on a Sunday in our back parking lot at church. The tears rise quickly. You are birthing something and it's emotional. I have so many different feelings. I shame myself a bit when I feel anything but excitement. Almost as if I can't have any negative feelings because I chose to let you do this through me. Did I? Could I have stopped you? I don't want to stop you. I trust you.

I remember the day you showed me the tree and all the leaves as people's names I wouldn't know. You promised and you were faithful.

It's an awkward month. It's like I'm pregnant but can't tell anyone. I told my closest friends but it's too soon to go public. Help me hold this good news with simple faith and joy while I continue to process what it might mean for me and our community.

God, I will not be distracted. You're changing my heart and giving me the ability to focus and follow-through. This is huge!

In the name of your son Jesus Christ, I resist the powers that try to scare me. They're not true. They don't have the truth. You do. I do. You are here. You are with me. While I wait.

January 10, 2018

What do you do when something is being birthed through you? You do less. You're gentle with yourself. You rest. The vision has energy reserves to grow. Less manipulation and busy work from me. More growth from God.

You expect fear and doubt. You're not surprised when they surface in unexpected ways.

You expect others to forget. Vision leaks. You hold it closer and deeper than everyone else. It feels lonely at times. You remind people of the new thing emerging.

You feel emotional. Because the new thing that's emerging for others first has to go through you. Which means you are changing. Letting go of more and more so you can be filled with something new.

You allow mixed feelings. Excitement, adrenaline, joy, fear, anxiety, doubt. Somehow they all mix and make your stomach feel like it might implode. But what if the work of God gives you a stomach ache? Do you wish it away? Go back to life as usual?

I am so used to avoiding anything that feels like anxiety. To walk into it on purpose is far beyond anything I thought I could ever do.

You keep opening your hands, over and over and over. Because you aren't in charge anyways. And when something this big is birthed through you, you quickly learn what requires your attention while everything else fades away. There's so much you don't need to know. It's quite staggering how focused you are on the biggest part of this vision. You don't need to know details really at all. You're focused on making sure you can simplify this vision as much as possible and paint a picture of what could be. Details will come.

You're focused on caring for your church and walking with them as they encounter a new possibility.

You take a risk and stand up and throw seeds all over the place to prepare your community to birth the vision through them. You find deep delight in knowing why you share what you share when you share it. And trust that people will know more when the time is right. You feel content that moment is not today.

You aren't surprised when the vision doesn't feel as exciting as it did at the beginning. You make the time to remember and refresh and reconnect with the importance of the vision. You remember what you saw at the beginning and affirm it's still true.

You get distracted for moments or days. Evil would love to see you distracted. But then you remember in one glorious second that this thing is going somewhere on purpose and you can breathe deep again. It puts everything else in perspective. No more bursting energy driving us in 15 directions. One image, one story, one vision is calling us in that direction. We won't get there in a straight line on a direct route. It's your job to point others in that direction.

You learn again and again whose vision this is. You get the honor of seeing it for a moment. But this is God's idea of what's possible. Freedom.

You expect it to feel fuzzy to others at first. You resist the desire to clarify everything. Allow them to struggle with the ambiguity too.

You make space to realize again and again this vision could never be controlled. It can never fit into what you fully understand. It will always be bigger than your box, your perspective, your calendar, your sermon series planning. This used to feel stressful and anxious. Now you feel freer than ever before. You don't have to control this! Someone else holds it all. You merely open a few doors in the community and God gets to work.

Six months into the vision, a new team is unleashed and you realize how spiritually tired you are. This is heavy lifting, even though it felt light at times. An intentional season of rest and filling up is required. You try to trust the rhythm will be whole on the other side, even when you feel drained and poured out.

I want to make peace with the truth that I'm about to introduce tension into my community. As someone who craves balance and calm and peace, I'm about to upset the fruit basket in the name of Jesus.

Ugh.

January 15, 2018

What story do I need to tell today?

I am entering a season of leadership where I will have countless opportunities to hold on tight and control a new thing being born. I will want to name it, form it, pick out clothes, make a baby registry, and set the agenda for what this thing will become. But that is not my job. My job is to help call and invite the thing into existence. To prepare this community to give birth. We are co-creators with you, God.

I want to commit to a meditation practice of 20 minutes in the morning and 20 minutes in the evening. Without a renewed focus in meditation, I am at risk of killing the thing I want to help create.

The very moment I sense I want to hold on tighter, is the very moment I must do whatever I can to let go.

And maybe that's exactly what's been happening this month. We came back from vacation and my behaviors looked like surrender. My language sounded like surrender. But am I still holding on too tightly? Or am I surrendered to this vision, but it still feels big and out of control so I'm trying to control things around it?

I haven't experienced it in this way before. I thought because I looked and felt surrendered, that I was. But I suspect, as I get deeper into life, my letting go and surrender will be nuanced and subtle. With anxiety and panic, it was clear where I was holding too tightly. But now? It's subtle. Quiet. The control hides. Like a six-year-old playing hide and seek with me. She's now able to find a spot and stay fairly quiet. The three-year-old still giggles and shrieks the location of his clever hiding spot under a small pillow. But oh the six-year-old. She is smart, sophisticated, tricky. The six-year-old finds a hiding spot where it takes some work to find her.

My control is getting more sophisticated. This means my paying attention skills will need to develop and mature. Cue: deeper meditation practice.

What do you do when your new behaviors trick you into thinking you've "mastered something?"

January 23, 2018

Thank you for clarity. For vision. For a picture of what to move closer to. It helps so much on the days when I feel distracted. I see you inviting us to build bridges in our community. So people can cross both ways. What communities need a new bridge?

We could kick rocks and sticks around for years and feel like we're doing something for you. I don't want to just stack the wood for you, God. I want to get the people with the right tools and hearts and skills in the right places. I want to free them to do what they were made to do. I want to cheer you on as you move in your people. Let's build some actual bridges.

Your vision is such a gift. I'm holding your gift differently than before. Earlier, I would have acted like I was holding it lightly, but inside I was holding an idea with every ounce of energy I had. The idea defined me. It meant I was worthy, a good leader, that I belonged.

But this vision? I'm holding it lightly. It doesn't need me to suck the life out of it. It's bigger than anything I could hold anyways. It has a life of its own. I get to steward it. It's like the vision is a newborn child and I get to help keep it alive with the basics. But this vision has its own life-force. It's not an extension of me. It was simply born through me.

Your vision doesn't feel heavy. It's not a huge thing to manage and figure out and plan. Which is a beautiful gift in itself. I'm learning how to hold your gifts differently. Joy!

I got a glimpse of the story you want to write in Marysville, of the bridges you want to build, and I'm willing to deliver the story to your people so they can make room for you to do what you do best!

None of the insecurity from other ideas/visions/possibilities is tied up in this one. Why is that? I am surprised it shifted so fast. The other ones were simply not the right ones for us. This vision? It came straight from your heart. That's crazy to type that. But it feels true.

February 3, 2018

Most of my life has been pointing towards today for the last couple of months. It's our Dreaming Session with church leaders and our Innovation and Vitality Team. It's here! I feel excited. A little nervous. You are birthing something through these people and I'm here to help shepherd it through.

We give you all of today. All the details, reactions, dynamics, words, stories, next steps.

God, I trust you with everything I am. Today is for you. Thank you for teaching me how to let go. It's such a more compelling way to live than before where I pretended to trust you but I trusted what I could produce. Today you'll produce something I could never do on my own. This is freedom.

God, help me enjoy today. You're here. You've got room to work. Do your thing!

February 5, 2018

Thank you. God, you are faithful. Saturday went well. People felt stretched, challenged, and excited. The energy in the room simmered beautifully. I hope they're open and receiving your vision in them.

I sat in the sanctuary after and felt you whisper, "Wait." I got in the car later and said, "Seriously God? More waiting?!"

But that's the rhythm isn't it? This adventure will never get me steps 3-10. I've got step 1 and 2. I grew so much from having time with the vision. I want them to have that sacred time too.

God we are yours. Do your thing in us!

May 12, 2020

Fast forward two years later and Kate, our church planter, is facilitating Better Together, a new faith community in Marysville. Just as we started to lean into possibilities for the next expression, I was asked to serve Edmonds. Curiously enough, I don't feel released from this vision. I wonder how it will continue to speak in our area. I wonder if Edmonds will feel a stirring to multiply in new ways.

I wonder if God will inspire the people of Marysville United Methodist Church in a new and different direction. I'll fully support any new discernment that arises. This was never my vision. 10 in 30 was a vision of what could be through a people in a specific time and place.

I open my hands and release any outcomes we hoped and planned for. God is leading and as long as we wrestle, listen, and trust, we'll be right where we need to be.

Saying Yes First

I want my life to shift before I say yes
Before I risk
jump
trust

I want to see the plans
Steps one through ten
rolled out on the table
with a pencil over my ear
and biting my lip a bit

I want to analyze
Get my thoughts in order
Make sense of it all

I want to feel how the
new thing will feel

Then I'll say yes
But what if saying yes first
Opening up to a new maybe
Letting go of control
Triggers the shift?

What am I missing out on
because
I can't
bring myself

to say yes
first?

> "Wesley, let's dance. You don't have to but I might make you."

— ISABELLA

8

DEEP WATERS

A Bag of Rocks | January 4, 2018

S ome days I look around at the world and see each of us holding a bag of rocks. We've each got something we're holding that's hurt us in the past. A deep wound where someone hurt us to the core of who we are. It may have been an accident or on purpose, but we've got these rocks. These wounds. And we're afraid of them.

I recently came across this quote. No author was attached.

"Your wound is probably not your fault, but your healing is your responsibility."

We're all walking wounded. We're holding something that just about did us in. And if we got quiet enough and allow the pain to rise, we fear we'd be done. We wouldn't make it. The pain and fear would get us.

We hold shame over our wounds. We could have stopped it. We wonder if it's our fault. Did we bring it on ourselves? Shame might as well be a shovel at the beach. When shame is the loudest voice we listen to, we're digging ourselves a hole. We'll bury ourselves alive with the voice of shame. It's brutal. "You should have..." "Why didn't you..." "Who do you think you are..."

I'd love to pull you quietly aside, take the shovel, and whisper, "Those voices aren't true." If you could see the voices of shame for what they are...fear...then maybe you could see them in a new light.

Once you stop believing the shame, it starts to lose its power. When shame starts to lose its power, oh dear friend. Watch out. Things are about to get so good.

Then you might be ready to take responsibility for healing. To stop blaming yourself for a deep wound that you probably didn't inflict upon yourself. Someone else did. They were hurt and they hurt you.

Your healing is your journey to make. Your resurrection is calling you. The One who made you has this fascinating ability to love you right now and hold a vision of what you could become.

What if you're holding something heavy but don't realize it? What if you could set down the bag of rocks? Would you?

Freedom is whispering your name, my friend. In this new year, allow yourself to receive the best gift you could receive. Your healing.

Strength | February 2, 2018

Yesterday I was thinking about inner strength vs. external circumstances. My peace used to be based on the situation around me. I was always ready to react to people, decisions, facial expressions around me. The stronger power lay outside of me. My insides were at the mercy of my outsides. Nothing inside felt very grounded. It could change in an instant based on an email, a phone call, a new problem, a question from my child. It felt too uncertain inside.

This did not align with the peace and strength found in Christ. And when my behaviors don't match what I value, that dissonance causes anxiety.

Waking up and shining a light on my fear and anxiety helped me see this in a new way.

I feel a peace inside that's stronger than anything I've felt before. Feelings come and go. Situations come and go. People come and go. But whatever is inside of me doesn't waver. It knows a different story that's stronger than the passing stories.

 Wesley: "I told Dad it's okay to cry because crying is how you get your cry out."

Me: "You're right."

Wesley: "I'm always right."

After the Fact | February 4, 2018

I feel like I don't have a lot of practice trusting God with intention. I've called a lot of things "trust" when it felt more like I tried to control it but couldn't. *And after the fact, I tried to call that faith.*

Yes.

The Old Path

Something is shifting
I sense it
I'm sad but it's not dramatic

It's quiet
resolute
expectant
I knew this was coming

Stepping into a new adventure
asks new things of me
It's exciting
and sad
The old way made sense
The new way feels uncomfortable
awkward
unsure

I miss the old path
I knew it's twists and turns
I knew the outcomes

And yet

You are present in the new thing
I look behind and see your faithfulness
I look ahead and see your faithfulness
Holding out your hand with
a smile on your face

You know what's to come
I do not

Am I willing to give up what I know to
follow you to where I don't?

I know the excitement of a new adventure

God, keep extending your hand to me from the new path

I'll follow
Stay close
I'm letting go of a lot
I need you

A Whole New World | February 10, 2018

I don't like it when I'm sad and need to cry and don't know why. Yes, sure God, you're growing me and things are shifting and I'm letting go of a lot and opening myself up to a huge season of not knowing. But I still expect that I know what my new feelings are so that I can "fix" them.

I'm in a whole new reality. How do I get the lay of the land when I've never been here before?

My life feels wildly disrupted *and* eerily calm. It's an unsettling combination.

This is why I keep going about my life like it's normal but there's so much emotion right under the surface. I don't know how to move through this new life yet. There's no autopilot. I don't want autopilot. But it's familiar.

I'm still surprised that I don't get to go back to life as normal.

Now that I've seen where we could go, I don't want to go back. I'm stuck in the middle. Can't go back. Can't go as far forward as I'd like to some days.

I'm in a whole new world. But I expect it to feel like my old one.

When I'm in the midst of Sunday mornings and gathering with people, I feel grounded, excited, and fully present. This enables me to lead in a way that feels good. I don't feel scared or anxious. I feel led.

It's the in-between days, the quiet space, where I don't feel as grounded. I don't feel anxious. It's different than before. But I don't see the next steps of the path very clearly when I'm by myself. It feels weird. I'm used to sensing what was next. It challenges my desire to be in control. It's interesting that clarity comes through community.

It's not my default to trust you yet God. I do after a bit of searching and wondering and building my piece of solid ground. But God, I can't build solid ground that lasts. Searching for that leads to suffering and is a waste of time.

God, you showed me part of the future. Now the present doesn't feel as captivating. But this is where I live. I don't live in the future. You're teaching me to stretch and think about the future so we can make room for something meaningful. But I'm not used to it yet. I'm used to living in the present or the past. Fascinating.

The Day My Phone Died

The other day my phone died
I laughed to cover up the fear
What would I do without my phone?
That message couldn't go out
That picture couldn't be taken
My throat grew tight as I wondered
What would I do if there was a fire
An accident
A question
Silence

What would I do with silence?

Every few minutes I saw my hands
Reach for my phone
I laughed to cover up the fear

What is wrong with me that
I can't live without my phone?
The 90 minutes without my phone
Taught me more than I wanted
To know about myself
That day.

Susan & Lisa's Wedding Day | February 17, 2018

Sometimes we qualify love. We say it looks like this or that. We put love in a box and define it for others. But love can never be contained. It's too big and strong to be told what to do. Love patiently ignores any attempt to color inside perceived lines. Love fills the whole page with rich and beautiful color. The color bursts forth as if to say, "See what you were missing when you thought love only looked like this or that?"

Love shouts and whispers to the world, "Look. See this. This is what love looks like."

Jesus lived a life of love. From him we learn characteristics that will help us greatly in all of our marriages.

Patience: Cut each other some slack. Be gracious. Forgive and move on.

Service: You are to serve each other. To take care of each other.

Sacrifice: Jesus gave up his life so we could be in a relationship with God. Sacrifice in marriage. Yield to each other. Compromise.

Prayer: I encourage you to pray together and for each other. One of my friends ends each day by listening to his wife breathe as she falls asleep. He thanks God for her each night. God will guide you through good and hard times with grace and peace.

Most of all, love. Love each other well. Be the first to hug and kiss after an argument. Give each other kind words. And share that love with the world. It is a testament to how much God loves you. Love always protects, always trusts, always hopes, always perseveres. We are honored to witness your love today. May your love and commitment continue to deepen as you journey through life together.

One of God's gifts was breathing life into humans and turning them toward each other to live in equality and unity. Susan and Lisa have come to affirm their love for each other and enter into this sacred union. Christ calls you into union with him and with one another. I ask you now in the presence of God and these people to declare your intention.

"Susan, do you take this woman to be your wife, to live together in a holy marriage? Do you promise to love her, comfort her, honor and keep her in sickness and in health, and forsaking all others, be faithful to her as long as you both shall live? If so, say I do."

"I do."

"Lisa, do you take this woman to be your wife, to live together in a holy marriage? Do you promise to love her, comfort her, honor and keep her in sickness and in health, and forsaking all others, be faithful to her as long as you both shall live? If so, say I do."

"I do."

Amen.

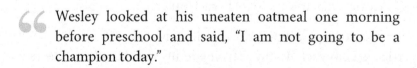

Wesley looked at his uneaten oatmeal one morning before preschool and said, "I am not going to be a champion today."

Boring | April 9, 2018

What do you do when the long, slow, miraculous work of God feels boring? I've always moved on before. Not anymore. I want the long, slow, boring miracle that happens so slowly you hardly notice. These are the miracles that last.

God is calling me to miracles that last. They might not look as exciting as I previously thought.

 "Mom, I want to feel comfortable *now!*"

— ISABELLA, AFTER AN ANXIOUS FIRST DAY OF SCHOOL

Marlene Rose | May 14, 2018

On a Monday morning in mid-May, I finshed up a meeting with Kate in the church office. My daughter was right down the road at kindergarten, playing her heart out. It was 2:25 pm. I got a text message to meet a family at the hospital. They wanted to pray together as their mother was not expected to live much longer.

I walked into the room at 2:41 pm. The family was standing around Marlene's bed. I heard a nurse quietly talking as she gave morphine. Sounds of sniffling and tears filled the room as light streamed in. A grandson rushed in the door, getting there just in time. One of the granddaughters leaned over to me and shared that her grandmother had taken a turn. Marlene's breathing changed and the end felt near.

Her son turned and saw me by the door and said, "Oh good, Jenny is here!" He seemed happy to see me. I walked over to the head of her bed. I put my hands on her head and shoulders and asked the family if it was okay to pray. Yeses filled the room. I started to pray. To thank God for this beloved woman's long and beautiful life. To remind her she was loved and her family would be okay. To comfort her as she let go. To be with the family as they let go. We thanked God for this gracious gift of life. As we told her it was okay to go, she took one last breath and went still.

We stopped praying and looked at each other. Through tears, I gave a small smile to the family. We looked at each other incredulously. Did that just happen? Did we pray her into the arms of God?

I wiped away my tears, gave a few hugs, and gave the family their space to say goodbye. As I stepped into the hallway, I glanced at my phone and realized it was 3:20 pm. Time to pick up my daughter from school. In 40 minutes, I went from praying with someone as she took her last breath to now sitting in the school pick up line. Wow.

It is a holy privilege when pastors are invited into some of the most sacred moments of people's lives. We stand before two people and declare they are partners in the eyes of God. We rub ashes on people's foreheads and remind them they came from dust and to dust they'll return. We hold a cup and bread and remind them God loves them more than they might ever understand. We hold a hand while someone waits for their loved one in surgery. We place our hands on someone's head as we declare they are a child of God and the water runs down their face.

We tell people God loves them. All the time. In any way we can think of. It's a pretty fantastic job.

I walked in the door at home and knelt on the floor to say hi to three-year-old Wesley. "I got to pray with someone who was sick and then she went to be with Jesus today." He looked away from his legos and over at me. "Well, I built a volcano!"

Yup. Sounds about right. All of it is sacred and holy.

———

Let Me Lead

I hear you, God
Loud and clear
You want to lead
I get it
But I want to lead too
It's how you made me
I want to call the shots
Take the first step
Point the way for others

You keep whispering,
"Let me lead."

I'll try to listen
And let you lead

Your voice is growing louder
And louder
And louder

Allow | May 20, 2018

I want to be a life-giver. Which means I'm invited to walk into spaces of death and stagnation and speak life. I can't get one without the other.

This happens when I pray with someone as they pass. When I'm telling someone they're not right for a position. When I help a ministry see a new way forward.

I am bringing life. But not *my* life. My life cracks open space for God to bring life. I'm preparing the space.

And this takes energy, care of self, and groundedness in my true role for this to be sustainable.

God, you're the one moving things and people and hearts around. I said yes to showing up. I get to *allow*.

Nothing to Protect | June 20, 2018

Anxiety made me believe I had something to protect. At all costs, I would make sure I had everything taken care of. I would know what to do in every situation. I would be good at everything. I would be safe. Anxiety made me believe all the worry, agendas, fear, manipulation and frantic high-functioning was necessary.

I'm realizing there's not much to protect. What's underneath doesn't need protection. It's strong, simple, clear. It simply is.

Freedom.

Train Wrecks

Some days feel like a train wreck
Nothing goes according to carefully laid plans
Agendas are ripped to shreds
Hours wasted
Resources thrown aside

Failure whispers
Failure wants attention
Failure tries to write the story

"Who do you think you are?"

"You'll never be good enough"
"You're a train wreck"

But what if the author of the true story
secretly loves train wrecks?

Not in a mean or vindictive way
but in a hope-filled clap your hands
kind of way?

When perfection falls apart
Love gets more room to work

When people react differently than planned
Grace gets more room to work

When no one follows their cue
or script
or intention
Spirit gets more room to work

Hard work still matters
Trying our best is still worthy
But the true story remains

God shines the most in train wrecks

Year Number Thirteen | July 3, 2018

"Maybe this won't work out."

It was a Thursday morning. Our young children were eating breakfast and playfully arguing over who got to look at the back of the cereal box.

My husband and I were around the corner in our home office. Him sitting on a chair with his arms crossed and eerily quiet. Me slumped against the back of the door. It was closed.

"What are you saying? That we should get a divorce?"

Silence.

Tears.

I heard my voice desperately ask a few more questions. This conversation wasn't going anywhere good at this point. But that wouldn't stop me from grasping at straws.

I launched into what I thought was a piercingly accurate description of what was going on. I sent the ball into his court. I set it up perfectly for him to say yes, that's all this is. We'll be fine.

Silence.

I stood up. I wiped my tears. I grabbed the door handle and quietly closed it behind me. I wanted to slam it but didn't want to upset our kids who had progressed to launching mini wheats into each other's cereal bowls.

Oh to be three and six years old.

I went through the motions that morning and got the kids ready for their day. I turned away from my husband as he left to take the kids to school. Anything to communicate how hurt and confused I was.

The garage door closed.

The house was quiet.

I sank into the couch.

And cried.

The pain and fear and desperation spilled out into the quiet room. I cried for the countless conversations that ended with slammed doors and chilling silence. Tears fell for the relationship that was so far from what we both knew it could be. Sobs erupted from the anger of not knowing how to fix this. Did I want to fix this?

Yes.

But how?

Fast forward four months later.

Here's what we're learning together.

Fear is a liar. When one person in a relationship relates to the world primarily through a lens of anxiety and panic, it will affect their deepest relationships in a profound and unseen way.

I worked my tail off in 2017 to get healthy when it comes to anxiety and panic. A year later, I'm only beginning to uncover how that fear-based way of living has sunk its claws into every element of my relationship with my husband. So I'm ever so slowly pulling back the covers and shining a light on the fear. Instead of finding my darkest worries, I am uncovering an entirely different way to see my marriage.

I have always been a fairly sensitive and tightly wound individual. But going to college, getting married, and moving 5000 miles away from what I knew caused something to unravel in me. I had my first panic attack five months after we got married. I was young and completely oblivious to the fear running through the foundation of my life. I am a bit of a perfectionist. I wanted my marriage to be wonderful. So I set about doing and being all the things I thought a good wife was.

And only now, in year thirteen, can I see that my husband was not getting my full self. I was not getting my full self. Fear caused me to live half alive.

As we've gone through photo albums, shared memories, and visited our old homes, pain and grief still knocks me over. My husband shares happy memories of those seasons of our life. Not me. Most of my memories had a third constant companion that numbed me to the moments. This unwelcome and unkind "friend" kept me in the corner, present but not fully alive.

Fear.

Fear and anxiety affected everything. At the time, I had no idea.

That is what enabled me to compartmentalize my marriage. I simply convinced myself that this was the one area in my life that I could never seem to get right. We would have a big argument and then reconnect and it felt like I had escaped the problem at least for a little while. I was always running. Trying to stay one step ahead so that I could convince my husband I was a good wife. Even while I was grasping at anything I could to help me understand why this cycle never ended.

I went to a counselor. He went to a counselor. We went to counseling together. We talked to a couple of trusted friends.

We were good parents. No matter what was happening, our kids knew they were loved and safe.

We continued to serve in a community of faith in significant leadership positions. We still loved each other. We were a great team. Things were okay. But we both knew they were far from what we wanted this relationship to be in this world.

Every relationship has its issues. So I never felt disingenuous while we worked together at our church to help create a community of grace and love for all people. Our love for these people and each other was so real and deep. But when life got quiet and I was alone, I allowed the difficult questions to surface.

What is it about me that is enabling the cycle to continue?

If I stop trying to "fix" him and look deeply at myself, would I see something that's not fully alive?

Where am I being self-centered?

Where are my habits hurting me or hurting those around me?

What way of seeing this relationship is tired and worn out?

What if this could be new? What would we value?

Do I love this person enough to do some really hard work?

One of the annoying things about following Jesus is how he helps me see something new about myself that might have been hurting me. The pain of seeing it, naming it, and then figuring out how to let it go and choose a new way is surprisingly difficult.

Jesus followers value dying to ourselves and following Christ. Giving myself to this rhythm over and over is no small undertaking.

One last question rumbled in my soul.

How do you remake a marriage while in progress? While little people run around expecting things like baths, dinner, and story time.

You let go.

For me, it happened in a million moments and all at once.

I was desperate. Nothing I could say or do seemed to fix anything, except kick the can down the road a few more weeks. I was done arguing and controlling and forcing outcomes. My husband has often been the one who was brave enough to ask the really hard question: What if this won't work out?

The question pierced my soul and I jumped into a hopeful positive mode every single time. Which meant I was ignoring the question.

Or more likely, I was ignoring his pain.

I sat in the back row at my Good Friday worship service. I listened to the story of Jesus being accused, convicted, and killed. I allowed myself to walk to the cross with him. A desperate whisper stirred in my soul.

Let it go.

It's time for someone else to hold this. Surrender.

That whisper alone cracked something open in me. I hated it at the same moment. As a Jesus follower and pastor, I encourage people to let go all the time. I think about it, I write about it, I read about it and I speak about it. And yet I am sometimes blind to the ways I am invited to let go.

I love the moment that I remember again this is the invitation of Jesus followers in the world. And I roll my eyes at the irony that somehow I forgot again.

Letting go feels like releasing your hands from a balloon filled with air. Everything you've been holding so tightly rushes out of you. It feels like freedom.

Letting go also feels like chasing the balloon that's now wildly twisting and turning in the air as it's released. You want to take it back and be in control.

From that moment on, I wish that I could tell you things got a lot easier and the next steps were obvious. It wasn't and they weren't.

But I was different. I had to keep letting go, over and over. But I was actually letting go. There is some saying about how we don't change our lives until the pain of staying the same is too much. It's true. We could have continued for decades with our marriage the way that it was. It was okay. It was even really good sometimes. But we were not fully alive with each other.

The grace is that my husband has been faithfully and consistently painting a vision that our marriage could be better for 13 years. My fear convinced me that I didn't know how to be a better wife or partner, so this was the best I could ever be. For over a decade, I set about convincing myself and him that this was as good as it gets.

Turns out he was right. Ugh. He's smiling right now, isn't he?

So now what? What if this was just another one of our cycles? Our muscle memory is prepared for this to go poorly in a few weeks.

But something is different.

What's left when I look under the fear? It's raw, scared, and real. It feels fragile but I can sense it's stronger than anything I've experienced before.

We've always said we want a new normal. We're finding it. In progress. While the kids are screaming in the backseat, throwing mud at the beach, refusing the food we've made, and resisting bath time.

The hugs and kisses mean something different now. The looks across the room say more than before. The soft smiles are sacred. The acts of kindness are infused with a deeper love and compassion.

We listen to each other better. We're learning to listen to what's said and what's left unsaid. We're letting go of old baggage in the ways we communicate. "The story I'm telling myself about what you're thinking is..." and we realize we're often wrong. We let the old habits go.

We call each other out gently when we feel ourselves slipping back into communication patterns that feel comfortable but we know they keep the bad cycle going.

We look at each other and see something new. Or rather, here's my confession. I see something new when I look at my husband. He's been looking at me like that for a long time and I didn't have eyes to see it or a heart to receive it.

Turns out anxiety and fear tried to protect me from many things. They also robbed me of countless moments of love, joy, and passion.

When I finally saw anxiety for the cruel and invisible pattern it was, it still took another year before I could see the destructive habits it pushed me into with those closest to me.

I recently had an experience with anxiety that illustrated how our first thirteen years were for Aaron. I noticed that when anxiety tightened my throat, my stomach churned, my breathing grew shallow and my thoughts stumbled around each other, my eyes laser-focused on myself or controlling the environments around our children. I didn't even see Aaron. He was physically there. But he might as well have been invisible to me.

The panic convinced me my only job was to save myself and the kids from whatever I had deemed unsafe and scary. Aaron was an adult. He could save himself. It was lonely for us both.

Turns out, a part of me wanted him to save me. But instead of showing vulnerability or any slight dependence on him, I simply threw up a wall and was determined to figure it out on my own.

Not my proudest pattern. But it's a very real one when it comes to survival skills and anxiety.

It makes me wonder today how he felt being invisible. I'm not sure he knew how little attention I could give him when I was anxious. He may have settled for the scraps for a while. But I imagine that loneliness birthed many of our arguments.

Anxiety and fear took so much of my energy. As I managed that monster, I also parented two young children, learned a new leadership role in my job, and navigated an anxiety-inducing presidential election and subsequent global crisis. I shouldn't be surprised that when my survival mode kicks in, I don't prioritize people in the best way.

How is it that the one person I wanted to love the best in the whole world was on the receiving end of my worst behavior?

I continue to reflect on this as our days move forward.

I will never be able to apologize enough or repair the incredible pain I caused my best friend by not dealing with my unhealthy patterns earlier.

He needed me for the last thirteen years and I couldn't get there. I didn't know how to show up to and for him.

As each layer of anxiety dissolves, what's underneath is exactly what he saw in me so long ago. I'm thankful for such a patient soul who helped me see it too.

God, I love this guy.

God has this ability to wake me up to what I've been sleeping through for far too long. I could have kept sleeping. No one would have noticed. But I knew. I knew I was asleep in my marriage. Just getting through. I understand this can be common for life with little ones. But it's not the life we want moving forward.

Here's to waking up to what's right in front of you. Especially the people you're closest to. Let's do the work on ourselves so we can show up more healthy and whole to our most favorite people in our world. This is what love does.

So here's a question for you, my friends:

What are you willing to look at, that could change everything?

Look at it. Pull the covers back. Shine a light on the thing you fear the most. Question it. Talk about it. Invite God to help you see something new.

Freedom.

 "I was nervous for my swim lesson. But I did it anyways and felt better. It changed."

— WESLEY

Standing on the Shore

I stand on the shore again

The safe shore
The known rocks and sand
My feet feel supported
My body is content

But my heart is pulling me
like a toddler's hand
toward a water playground

Deeper water is calling
Singing
Twinkling with laughter

My heart trusts and jumps in

My body and mind panic
We can't swim!
What if?!

My heart lives for the deep
It's fully alive

But my body and mind turn back
for the shore as quick as they can

I stand on the shore again

My heart continues to
play in the deep

Maybe one day I'll be whole again

9

TRUST THE DYING

Surrender | July 7, 2018

T rust the dying.

Whenever I surrender, I'm invited to trust the dying. And I'm led to a deeper level of faith and trust.

God, what's dying in and around me that I'm not allowing? What is tired and wants to let go but I'm forcing it to hold on? Where are my clutching and desperate hands wasting energy when something is already dying?

Show me. I want to release it.

———

 I wrote a phrase on a whiteboard in the kitchen: "I am loved."

Wesley erased the last letter. It said: "I am love."

———

Renewal Leave | August 20, 2018

"Mom, can you turn up the slow?!" My three-year-old screeched. I smiled. We were driving somewhere and he believes he is Lightning McQueen.

"Wesley, did you mean, can I turn up the speed?"

"Um, yeah."

This summer I got to turn up the slow. This is my attempt to capture it in writing. Mostly for me to remember down the road. But also to leave a trail of bread crumbs as so many of us are figuring life out together. How do we handle the fast pace of our lives? With increasing technology, how are we making space for silence, friendship, and presence? How do we recharge and renew when our lives are so full?

Every four years, United Methodist clergy can take four weeks off paid as a renewal leave. Some take it. Many don't. It's tempting for pastors to feel their church couldn't go on without them for four weeks. But they can. And they should.

I spent months and months preparing for renewal leave. I worked with my coach to process my hang-ups and expectations for this season. I had a lot. Was I supposed to accomplish something specific? How would I know if it was successful? Could I stay off email and social media for four weeks? Could I rest and recharge while caring for a three and six-year-old?

What would I do?

You might roll your eyes at my questions. But remember, I'm a One on the Enneagram. Reformer, Perfectionist. In my brain, I am defined by what I do. You want me to take four weeks and not do anything?

Unheard of in my 36 years of life so far.

The questions rumbled: Who am I without my work? How do I relate to my family when work quiets down? How might I be different when I return? What could I practice in this kind of season that would be nearly impossible to learn in my normal life?

Three priorities emerged. I wanted to spend some time by myself, some time with just my husband and time with family. I booked a trip to Alaska and Oregon. We envisioned day trips from Marysville the rest of the time. I was set.

Then our nephew became critically ill. As I wrapped things up at work, my husband flew across the country to sit in a hospital room with his beloved family as they watched Graysen fight for his life. Graysen passed away. Within an hour of this news, we were booking flights to Ohio, canceling a flight to Alaska, and asking people to cover things at work.

I'll never forget my last staff meeting before flying cross country the next day with my kids. Our team looked at me and said, "We want you to take a week of bereavement leave and then an extra week of vacation to be with family. Then start your renewal leave. We'll cover everything." My eyes blinked back tears and my throat tightened with emotion. "But I'd be gone a long time." They nodded.

It was an astounding gift of grace that I will never forget. I took a deep breath, put up an away message on my email, and got on an airplane.

We arrived in Ohio, I spoke at Graysen's memorial service, we shared stories, cried, and laughed. The time together as family felt healing. A short while later, I chatted with my uncle about how renewal leave was shifting. He gifted me three things to think about practicing on leave:

- **No expectations.** They're too heavy to hold.
- **Become all eye.** Notice everything. The breeze, the warm sun, the sounds of my kids' voices.
- **Distrust all thoughts.** Let them go.

153

These were very helpful as I moved through my days.

We also practiced things like taking the most scenic route when it was time to drive somewhere. I rarely chose the most direct route on the interstate. The side roads were glorious and felt like an adventure.

Our mornings were slow. We didn't set an alarm more than 3-4 times the whole month. I still woke up at 6:30 am most mornings. I would quietly slip outside for a walk, to read, to journal, to talk and listen with God.

I set everything aside when I heard little feet come downstairs. They crawled up into my lap and we rocked.

Nature was dripping with heaven. Everywhere I looked, I breathed in the green leaves, the sun shining on the water, the bird that flew over-head. With fewer things begging for my attention, I was free to focus my gaze on God all around me.

I read a ton of books. Mostly fiction.

I stayed off social media (mostly) for four weeks. Very little email.

I ate breakfast by the water. Hiked and played outside.

We had dance parties in the playroom, ran through the sprinkler, colored, and rocked on the porch swing.

We went swimming. Isabella even started swimming on her own and at last count, she swam in ten different bodies of water this summer!

I cried. A lot. Pretty much anytime I was by myself and I turned on some music, tears sprang to my eyes. I didn't spend too much time worrying about why. I simply allowed the tears to warm my cheeks.

I discovered the poetry of Hafiz and soaked up his wisdom and wonder. He helped me know the joy and laughter of God.

I noticed a deafening lack of stress during renewal leave and spent time reflecting on how I relate to my work. I work hard at my job. Really hard. And I value Sabbath rest on Fridays and Saturdays. This means my pace on Sunday-Thursday can be intense. I reviewed the things we've worked on in the last three years as a church and was overcome with the magnitude of this list. It helped me see some things I want to shift as I move back into work mode. How can I hold the calling differently? I want my ministry to be sustainable for another 30 years. I want to feel fully alive in this work. These reflections invited me to see much deeper what was underneath a desire to work so hard. God helped me uncover some profound things I hadn't seen about myself in a long time, if ever.

I learned to trust the dying, even more, when it comes to death and resurrection. I restarted a consistent meditation practice and noticed immediate benefits in my attention to the present moment. I asked God a million questions and learned how to listen. I realized I don't need to hold things alone. They're too heavy that way. I realized I'm still trying to earn love when it's given so freely.

The lack of stress and expectations from anyone else made space for me to connect with God, myself, my husband, and my family in ways that can get chaotic during our normal rhythm. We loved it.

Yesterday, Isabella smiled and said, "Mom, the next time we'll get four weeks like this together, I'll be ten!" She's really appreciated the gift of this summer together. (Little did she know how many weeks we'd get at home during a pandemic a couple of years later.)

So how was renewal leave?

I noticed the warmth of the sun on my skin. I felt the breeze move through my hair. I noticed the sounds of my kids' laughter. I kissed my husband like I meant it. I rocked on my swing and listened to the world. I struggled some days with the slower pace and the lack of productivity. I cried by the water. I danced in the kitchen.

And it was enough.

For my 36th birthday, Aaron gave me two nights away at a cottage on a lake near our home. Just me. It was glorious that it came at the end of my leave. I originally had planned my alone time at the beginning. But this was the perfect way to reflect on this month. As my kayak paddle sliced through the cool morning water, my soul whispered, "it's time to go back."

Here I am. I'm still the same person, but my heart is new. And it turns out, that's probably the point of renewal leave. It was never about what I would do. It was always about remembering I have a heart. And living in that heart.

While I'm glad to offer a new heart to the people in my world, I'm most thankful for this relationship with the One who made me. May our connection be the source of all goodness in my life for years to come.

The Back Row | August 22, 2018

The audience fills the room. Chatter and anticipation meet and rise. The heavy curtains on stage are closed. The lights flash and then dim. Silence comes over the room. The performer for the evening walks to an opening in the thick red curtains. The crowd inhales in eagerness for what they're about to witness. She pulls the curtain back, takes a deep breath, and walks out into the hot lights. The bright lights blind the performer from seeing anything but light. After blinking a few times, she sees something shocking. The audience is full of people who look just like her. She blinks again and shakes her head a bit. Yup. They're still there.

She's performing for herself.

The show must go on so she launches into the outline for the evening. The audience is a tough one. They whisper, point, and laugh in a way that feels like junior high snickers. Some sit with crossed arms and disapproving faces. Still others bury their heads in their phones.

Whatever she's doing isn't enough.

Intermission arrives and she runs off stage. She sinks into an ugly green chair and throws her head in her hands. Tears roll down her hot cheeks. How could she go back out there? They saw right through her. Nothing was enough. The songs, the dance, the art, the moving speech. None of it could satisfy her audience that night. They wanted more.

A stagehand walks around the corner and taps her on the shoulder. "It seems most people have left. Everyone would understand if you didn't finish the show. Go home and take care of yourself. But I did want to let you know there's someone in the back row who stayed. You might want to go out and say hi."

She inhales sharply and rises to see who this faithful visitor might be.

It was God.

She walks down the stage steps and passes row after row. The ground rises as she nears the back row. God leans to the left and pats the next chair over.

Seriously? After that performance?

With nowhere else to be, she gingerly takes a seat next to...God?

"Sweet child. You have spent your life performing. Waiting for applause and smiles and rewards. It's never enough, is it? You get one and start chasing after the next.

I imagine it's exhausting. But you're used to it, aren't you?"

She nods with her head bowed. "It's all I know."

God leans down and a soft smile emerges. "What if I can teach you a different way? Would you take it?"

She whispers through the tears, "Yes, please. Show me. I don't want to get to the end of my life and still be chasing an Oscar for the performances I've given when you just wanted a lifetime of coffee dates with me."

The floodgates have opened. "God, you love me in a way that doesn't require any performance. It makes no sense. I've spent my life searching for applause, a grade, a positive evaluation...anything so I can measure myself...against myself. And all you do is smile. It's like none of this even matters to you."

God replies, "My child, I've got a seat with your name on it right here in the back row. It's yours if you want it. All you have to do is get off the stage. This is easier said than done. So really think about it."

"I imagine life on the stage is lonely. And not because you don't have incredible people around you, but because you only depend on yourself. You've been looking to the people around you for affirmation and validation that you're doing everything correctly. What a lonely road. To constantly be on stage, never letting yourself take a break. Living in fear of making a mistake."

God reaches out and gently touches her arm. "You can get off the stage anytime you want. A long time ago, you learned that if you did good things, you felt loved. It's not a bad thing. But it's not how my love works with you."

"You're loved and alive and worthy and fantastic before you get on stage. If you truly knew and felt this deep in your bones, then I think you'd enjoy your life a lot more. Because I've invited you to do some incredible things and spend time with wonderful people telling them about me. But you've got to get off the stage. There's nothing there for you. It wastes your energy and the gifts I've given you. You don't feel content after another success. It's empty."

Now God's on a roll. "I understand people praise and affirm you. The gifts I've given you are wonderful. That's what they're celebrating; your response to the generous gifts from me. Their praise is a gift, not an expectation or pressure. You can learn to receive the praise, graciously thank them and sink into the back row again with me.

Come tell me when someone has affirmed you. Maybe this will remind you that the praise is a gift, not pressure to do more."

God gets serious. "Child, you have accomplished a lot in the last three years. A lot. You're tired. You neglected your marriage. You're terrified it's all going to happen again when you go back to work. You're worried you'll jump on stage because that's where you know how to be. It makes sense to you. It's familiar. But you don't have to."

"That drive that's buried so deep in you that you have no earthly clue how to get to it so you can let me see? I can see it." She holds her knees and rocks gently while silent tears stream down and fall onto her lap.

"I can see you. I know when you started to think this way. I know the first moment you stepped onto the stage and genuinely believed this was the way to be loved and love others. I noticed it then. Then I watched it seep into every area of your life. Now, I watch as you overwhelm yourself regularly with every new idea that skips across your consciousness. All in the hopes that this one will be enough. That this new effort or project will finally satisfy the lion who lives in you. This lion pulls you on stage all the time. But it's never enough, is it?"

She can't speak. God knows her. It feels like freedom.

She allows herself to wonder silently. Can I trust this God? This being who knows everything about me and still loves me? It feels too good to be true.

And yet...

She knows that as she has slowly navigated other painful realities and beliefs in her life, this insatiable drive to perform and improve and achieve has continued to chase her. It is exhausting. She wants to rest. More than rest, she wants to be enough.

The problem is, she knows that she is enough. It's the moments the momentum and energy swell at work, that she takes off like a rocket. She can't quite tell if she's being chased by the lion who won't quit or being invited forward by Spirit.

Is she being chased or invited?

God interrupts her thoughts. "Daughter, I am inviting you forward. Excitement, energy, momentum, and new ideas are a gift from me. Enjoy them. Run with them! It brings me joy to watch you encourage others to draw closer to me. I love it."

"I also see the lion that pulls you on stage when you're not paying attention. So the answer is quite simple."

"Pay attention."

"Check in with me. Often. I will tell you if you're being chased or invited. Sit in the back row with me. I'll take you on adventures you never imagined."

She nods confidently. "I can do that."

"Okay, child. Do you want to continue the rest of the show?"

She shakes her head. "No. I think I'll head home for the night."

A Little Help | September 18, 2018

One early Sunday morning, a very sleepy four-year-old boy walked through my home office door and climbed onto my lap. He rubbed his eyes and yawned. He stretched and nestled against my body. He breathed deeply of this new morning. I kissed him on the forehead and drank in the moment. I know one day this will end.

Then as quickly as he entered, he sat up and said, "I'm ready to go downstairs." He hopped off my lap and walked out the door. His wobbly early morning stumble was gone. He was ready to face the day.

Sometimes we need help waking up.

God Needs So Little

One day God told me,
"I need so little of you
To do my work"
Ouch

Writing | October 2, 2018

You know what's terrifying for an Enneagram One who's seventeen years into her chosen career field? That annoying little voice inside her head that pops up once in a while and whispers, "Maybe being a pastor isn't the only thing you want to be." That voice doesn't get to see the light of day because of a million expectations and assumptions. I whispered that sentence aloud in a spiritual direction session recently while simultaneously squashing the emotion that emerged. No time to think about that. Sunday is coming. Your family needs your salary. There's nothing else. This is it.

And yet. I found myself wrapping up renewal leave during the summer of 2018 and sitting by Twin Lakes on a warm August afternoon with music in my ears and a blank notebook on my lap. I needed to make sense of the road I was traveling. I was learning so much, so quickly, that my brain and heart struggled to talk to each other. I started writing. Dreaming. Wondering.

An hour later, I put my pen down, took a deep breath, and couldn't believe what I was looking at. It was the outline of not one, not two, but three books. Books I knew I could write. Books I would enjoy writing. I smiled with the giddiness of a child getting ice cream after dinner. The little kid in me jumped for joy.

This.

Pay attention.

And like clockwork, other voices emerged from the shadows. *Who do you think you are? No one wants to read this. You don't have time for this. You don't know how to write a full book. Sermons are one thing, but a book? Ha. You'll fail.*

Those voices pushed me right back into the box I had so joyfully unpacked that afternoon by the lake. But as nudges go, this one was persistent. I mentioned it to my coach in our next call. "I'm feeling an invitation to write more intentionally. Maybe a book…" I held my breath and waited for the judgment, shame, and ridicule to rain down. But Julia is not my inner critic. She's a kind human who believes in me but also calls me on my BS. Julia did what great coaches do. She asked questions. The truth spilled out as if it had been there all along.

"I'm starting to see people on the other side of this now. When I was stuck deep in anxiety and fear, I couldn't access other people. I physically saw them and did my job the best I could, but I couldn't see them. Writing feels like a bridge. It's how I'm making sense of this journey into deeper wholeness. I wonder if there are people out there trying to put words to this too."

We talked about vocation. A strong feeling for a certain career or occupation. Becoming an ordained elder in the United Methodist Church is a vocation. I was ordained to serve and lead local churches as a life vocation. It's not a job I get to clock out of. It's an identity.

Terror danced around the edges because at first, I thought I was challenging all of that. This goes to show how black and white an Enneagram One's mind can be as the default. Nowhere in my psyche could I imagine I could be both a pastor *and* a writer. Julia asked why. Because there are plenty of pastors who write books. Upon further reflection, we noticed (again) that the people I listed were all male. I couldn't see a possible reality for me until I saw someone like me trying it too.

In the months to come, we talked through all kinds of things that bubbled up in response to this stirring within me. We slowly untangled the old tired beliefs that kept this new identity from growing up. In one call, Julia asked, "What does it mean to be a pastor who writes? What does it mean to be a writer who pastors?"

We talked about failure. We went deep into the difficulty of self-promotion and increasing public attention. I was terrified of putting myself out there for all the reasons that cause women to pull back. We're taught our entire lives to play small and cheer on others. If we decide to say yes to that voice inside reminding us we're not our full self, we'll be torn down by other women. We're all playing this awful game because it's the only one we learned. Somewhere along the way, I decided the stirring was more important than the game.

We talked about how my vocation evolved when I became a wife and then a mother. It was bumpy and awkward. I had a sense of clarity that those things were good steps at the time. Writing feels the same. It's bumpy, awkward, and the next right thing. But how would it fit with being a pastor?

Julia laughed at me (kindly) one day when I wondered aloud, "I feel like I'm still fighting this invitation to write." She said, "This is a natural evolution of your ministry and yes, you're fighting it. But you're fighting it by doing it. You're writing a book proposal, building a writing community, and talking to an editor. You're deepening this vocation while your superego beats you up about it."

Yes to that. That felt real. I suddenly saw what was going on. I'd been asking friend after friend after friend to tell me it was worth it to write a book. I thought maybe one more voice would convince me to take the risk. Julia ended our call that day with the statement, "Jenny, write the damn book." I thought that would certainly open the floodgates of confidence. Nope. This was an inside job.

My inner critic continued to rage on. Even while I did the thing my heart knew was mine to do. It was a confusing time. My heart goes out to anyone who was in a relationship with me in the fall of 2018. I found a way to work it into every sentence. I was desperately looking for affirmation while I underwent a sizable identity shift in my soul.

I wanted to be a writing pastor. Or a pastor who writes. Either way was fine. And each time I circled back around to that deep knowing, it dug up story after story that lurked in my shadows.

When you say yes to a holy invitation to something your heart wants, it's also wrapped up in fear. If I wanted the beautiful thing on the inside, I'd have to enter into the fear. Again.

In the months to come, I uncovered all kinds of old storylines keeping me small. Masculine and feminine energy in leadership. Ways of being I picked up in my family of origin. Fear of taking up too much space. False beliefs about writers being the ones who've figured everything out. I walked gently through each of these like they were wildflowers in a field. I picked one at a time, looking at it from every angle and wondered what it had to teach me. The reckoning was real. Some flowers took one conversation to unravel. Others took months.

I met Christianne, a spiritual director and book editor, who ran Bookwifery at the time. Her goal was to help authors birth their books without losing their souls. I was all in! Through coaching, training, and incredibly patient support, Christianne taught me everything she knew about writing, curating an online community, and the publishing industry. Her emails, video calls, and the Bookwifery community were my lifeline as I navigated a new world. Christianne understood when I hit seasons where I needed to pause projects. She welcomed me back with open arms when it was time to pick it back up. On a recent trip to Florida, we made time to meet in Orlando for brunch and it was like meeting a childhood friend. It's beautiful when the deepest part of our heart is seen by another human. Christianne is someone who sees the inner wisdom of people and invites it to come out and play. You would not be reading this book without her guidance and listening ear.

In the meantime, I defined my writing culture and posted it on the wall above my computer.

- **No rush:** Words will rise. Doors will open. Question the urgency.
- **No violence:** To words or myself. Give kindness to stories and they'll emerge. Don't take myself so seriously. Have fun!
- **Trust the process:** Go deep. Be honest. Get frustrated. Rest. Start again.

My growing and stretching into a writing pastor has been and still is a fitful one. I continue to fight it in small ways, even while I do it. In a sense, I am embodying the thing while also pushing it away. It's coming to life through me while my eyes are closed and refusing to look in the mirror.

And yet, here we are. You're holding a book. That I wrote! So maybe that holy invitation several years ago was real. Here's to the holy invitations we receive. May we have the courage to say yes, even when they invite us into the unknown. It's worth the journey.

Tug of War

I'm at war with something
A thing I'm trying to create
mold
form
bend to what I see

So I pick up my end of the rope
Find a good grip and tug

There's resistance

Tightness
An unrelenting tension
I glare at the ground
as my shoes dig into the dirt

My hands ache and burn
Sweat drips to the earth
In desperation I look up
and see a surprising sight

The thing smiles
Right at me

And drops the rope

I fly backwards with
embarrassment and confusion
resentment and anger
I prop myself up and look at
the thing
Still smiling
An irritatingly truthful and honest
smile

Then she whispers,
My child.
I want to exist through you
You are one I've chosen
To partner with in this world

But I need you to
stop tugging at me

Let me be
Make space and I will emerge

When I'm ready

While you wait and practice patience
Work on yourself
Untangle your tapes
Your limiting beliefs
Your hang ups
And when I sense it's
Safe enough to meet you,
I will.
I promise.

My Whole Self | October 18, 2018

I think most of us want to live from our whole self, but we're not sure what that means or where all the parts went. Did you leave one on the floor back in high school when that person broke your heart? Is another part of you stuck back in 2001 watching the illusion of safety fall apart in our world as planes hit buildings? Maybe a piece of you was left in your childhood when someone hurt you.

For me, a part of myself was left on the floor when I was five years old. I grew up in an idyllic suburban Ohio neighborhood. Nice homes, well-kept sidewalks, and a big backyard full of climbing structures built by my dad. We even had a zip-line! My dad was a pastor and my mom was a nurse who chose to stay at home with my three younger siblings and me. (By the way, there's just about everything you need to know about me: I'm the oldest of four!)

Something happened when I was five. I don't know what it is. It wasn't physical or emotional abuse. When I hear stories of tragic childhoods, I'm overwhelmed by the positivity of my childhood. The voices whisper, "Who are you to have problems from your child-hood? It was pretty wonderful. You had pink headbands, food, a coloring desk, love, belonging, and a zip-line. Life was not traumatic for you."

True. And yet. Something happened when I was five. I came to believe I wasn't safe. I'm sure it was a minor incident. I got scared and didn't have the language for what I was feeling. I began an awkward partnership with fear. In a way, we became friends. It was a weird friendship. We spent a lot of time together. Played on the swings and talked. Fear whispered to me during class. Passed me notes. Walked with me down the school hallway. Fear went home with me and tried to get my attention while I played with my family. Fear wanted my attention the most as the darkness of night closed in. I would lay in bed as a young child and worry. Thought after thought after thought, tumbling over themselves, for my attention.

My daughter is six as I type this in the dark early morning hours in a hotel on Lopez Island in the San Juan Islands. I listen to her beautiful breathing (which yes, I already checked once this morning), and I think about the fear that already has befriended her. She likely doesn't have language yet for how she's living half alive. But in a way, she already is. She chose the short straw: the first-born daughter of an anxious mom with panic attacks. I've sat in several therapy sessions working through the guilt I have about how she sensed my fear at such an early age.

As I navigated crippling anxiety and panic, I remember holding her six-month-old body to my chest and rocking her while sobbing quiet tears. I told myself she couldn't tell because I was quiet. But bodies know the spirit in another body. We sense fear or calm. Hatred or joy. Our bodies are smarter than our minds most days. Some days, I still cry for the energy she sensed in me in her early years.

I'm grateful now that she is learning along with me to live from her whole self. I realize she still has junior high insecurity, high school dating, career uncertainty ahead of her, and plenty of time to figure out her friendship with fear. But because she is my daughter, she will get every tool in the book on how to navigate that tricky friendship.

You better believe we practice meditation, yoga, tapping, naming emotions, and talking about our feelings. It's pretty fascinating to watch a six-year-old come home from a trying day at school and say through tears, "Mom, I feel upset. I'm worried about getting an award at school." We name her fear and allow it to be in the space between us. We witness it. We don't banish it away in shame and darkness. Fear is normal. It's allowed to be here. But it doesn't get to drive.

So feeling by feeling, my daughter is learning to live from her whole self.

So am I.

When we slowly pick through the memories of our life and enter into the pain with compassion and gentleness, we allow the different pieces of us to move toward healing. Then we get to put those pieces back together in a new mosaic.

I remember one day, about a month after "my waking up," I sat on a chair at a conference center on the Puget Sound. The blue water glistened, a bird flew by and my heart was experiencing a strange new calmness. I felt my fingers type out the beginnings of my Easter message that I would eventually share a month or two later. I wrote, "Resurrection watches the pieces of your life become beautifully dismantled. Pieces of the you you've always been are lying on the floor and it's simply beautiful. It takes your breath away when you realize you don't need those pieces anymore."

We might think becoming whole means every piece of us needs to come back together, even the damaged and painful pieces. The truth is that we're invited to pick up each piece and hold it in the light. We turn it around in our hands. We remember, honor, celebrate, grieve, and wonder. Then we pick the ones that make us feel alive and put them together in a new image. This is how we become whole. We're not afraid of the damaged pieces. We can become deeply thankful they were a part of our lives.

Fear became my friend when I was five. Fear is no longer my friend. I see it. I don't deny it. I'm fully aware of its desire to be my friend. It's like fear keeps sending me Friend Requests on Facebook and I think about it for a few days.

And then I hit Decline.

 "Mom, I've been holding in my tears for a few nights."

— Isabella

Allowing Tears

Tears used to accompany judgment
"Hold it together"
"What's wrong with you?"
"Something else to fix"

A story emerged with the tears
of criticism
confusion
shame

But what if tears are rarely something to fix?

Maybe tears are simply an indicator
instead of shutting them down
you allow them to flow
as a sign that you are
fully alive
in this moment

Regardless of the story about your pain
The tears are there
They want to be felt
To be seen
Noticed
Witnessed

Tears are not a statement
on what you should or should not be feeling

Tears are truth
of what's on the inside
that's desperately longing
to be felt
on the outside

May your tears be invited to trickle
down warm cheeks
when they arrive

Something lies on the other
side of tears
that you can't get to without
welcoming them to the surface

Palms Up Manifesto | October 29, 2018

On a warm and beautiful October afternoon, I took my laptop outside to the backyard. The leaves fluttered and a few fell to the ground as I wrote a piece about the kind of world I hoped would exist one day. Fifteen minutes later, I stopped typing and took a deep breath of gratitude. Then hit publish on my blog. Let's become the leaders our world needs.

A Manifesto For a Palms Up Leader

We show up.
When it's convenient and when it's difficult.
We willingly place ourselves in brave spaces so others can feel
*   brave too.*
We know grace and love will rise in moments of vulnerability
*   and honesty.*

We choose to unclench our fists from proven strategies and
*   past successes.*
We relax our tense shoulders and release control of outcomes.
We open our palms to the sky in tentative courage,
So that wisdom and plans and joy can enter, then leave and
*   enter again.*

We take care of ourselves first so we can care for others.
We don't just say that. We actually do it.
We shut down our computers and phones and step away to rest
*   and play.*
Our families know our hugs, feelings, and laughter.
They see our eyes.

We collaborate with and encourage our colleagues.
We know there's no such thing as competition among us.
It's an old story that we're ready to let igo.
We need every single one of us in the game, fully alive, and
*   ready to go.*

We have nothing to prove.
We are not defined by our metrics and numbers and stats.
Our worth isn't hidden in our latest greatest idea.
We are already loved.
We create out of joy, delight, and holy necessity.

We go to therapy. We have spiritual directors.
We might even have a coach. We have friends.
We have listening ears we trust with the truest parts of our
*   story.*
We build a team of people who shine a light for us so we can
*   shine a light for others.*

We read, listen, and meet the experts in our field.
We're thankful for the wisdom they pass on.
But we know nothing can replace what we sense and see in our
*   actual context.*
We're practicing, every single day, listening to a deeper voice
*   of wisdom*
That shows us the next step, when we get quiet enough to
*   listen.*

We are here to help others fly. To be fully alive.
We see a spark in people that no one else might see.
We name it, call it out of hiding, stir up possibilities and point
*   people toward God.*
We build teams who trust each other, love their work and do
*   things better than us.*

We ask questions in places we assume we know the answers.
We resist the voice that tells us we should know all the
*   answers.*
We give away power to others we come to trust
And we give them permission to question us. We're on the
*   same team.*

We don't hold anything alone.
We'll think we do. But we don't.
Our communities want to hold the heavy things with us if
*   we'll let them.*
Maybe it's been heavy because we've been holding something

We were never meant to hold alone.

We say no to good ideas.
We say no to things not meant for us in this season.
We say no to obligations, control, and unspoken expectations.
We say no to cynicism, isolation, and triangulations.

We say yes to ideas that shimmer with the holy.
We say yes to celebration and curiosity.
We say yes to moving at a slower rhythm and pace.
We say yes to dreams so big we could never make them happen
  on our own.

We trust God in each other. We're not bringing Spirit to
  anyone.

Love is already here. It's not surprised to see us.
It's glad to see we cooperated and showed up.
And Love knows if we don't show up, someone else will.
We know it's okay to not love everyone that needs loving.
We're the body of Christ. We're in this together.

Most of all, we are people who move through life with open
  palms.
We are surrendering our control over people and plans.
We are learning to let go of agendas and manipulation and
  fear.
We are leaders who are dancing in the truth that the pressure
  is off.

The rule book has been thrown out.
We know we're not in charge anymore.
We've given our lives to listen to the One who will take us
Where we need to go.
It turns out it's where we wanted to go the whole time.

Shouting at Flowers | November 16, 2018

What does it feel like when your body and spirit long to be in a season of hibernation but you are pushing your body and spirit to bloom? To create and to produce? What damage is done to your spirit when your mind refuses to listen to what your spirit knows that it needs?

It feels like I'm shouting at a withering flower to bloom in January.

It isn't her time yet.

There is work I need to do under the surface of who I am that is *not* for anyone else's consumption right now. It is mine alone. And as someone who is such an open book, I have to fight my inclination to share my process and my becoming as it happens.

This book proposal is asking something of me that I don't know how to give yet. I'm so thankful for the invitation to another room in my heart that was closed.

 "Mom, I'm going to fly my drone and if it hits outer space, then Dad told me to press this button."

— Isabella

Would You Go?

The world is so beautiful
It's also full of awful
We don't want to get stuck
in only one or the other

If we only look at the beautiful

we miss the injustice we must
work to change
If we only look at the awful
we remain paralyzed under
half-truths that convince us
we're stuck
"That's just how it is."

But what if it's not just how it is?

What if beauty and grace and love and freedom
are found right in the middle of the awful and the beautiful?
Would you go there?

10

YOU'RE INVITED

Reckoning with Church Growth | November 18, 2018

One winter afternoon in my first pastoral appointment, I sat in my senior pastor's office and he asked me what kind of pastoral leader I wanted to be. If I could do anything, what work would I find life-giving? This was 2011. I answered, "I'm fascinated by large church systems. I'm curious about how someone casts vision, organizes systems, and helps a group of people do something beautiful in the world. And I'm endlessly curious about how we communicate love and grace to people who are done with the church. I wish I could have one foot in the existing church and one foot in the rest of the world."

I'm still surprised that I was surprised by the 10 in 30 vision that arrived six years later. It was an answer to my heart's consistent cry to nurture healthy existing churches while experimenting with new ways of being church. Yet, in the middle of that dance comes a woman, in her 30s, trying to reconcile the leadership rules she'd been handed. Mind you, these were never given out in a public way. They were silently communicated through hallway conversations with colleagues and muttered in the Annual Conference peanut gallery. *This is how we do things. Women, stay small. Hang back. The men are in charge. Sure, some women have broken through but they'll pay a cost for that. Be faithful and dream big. But we could move you at any point. So don't rock the boat too much. We give you permission to fail. But your numbers better not go down on charge conference reports.*

Into that silent conversation, steps a young female pastor with a deep love for large church systems and innovating new ways of being church. I had no idea where I fit. Was it truly okay to innovate? I heard yes. But I was never quite sure my church wanted to. God built me this way, so I had to lean into the growth of all kinds. I have countless journal entries where I felt apologetic for growth. Surprise, surprise, my coach invited me to reflect a little deeper on why that might be. We uncovered several storylines that weren't serving me anymore.

The Grief of Growth

Church size dynamics teaches that for an organization to grow, it must break five (often painful) habits.

- They must let go of needing to know every person. This can be difficult when it feels like a church is getting too big and impersonal.
- Churches are invited to plan for the cost of additional staff. A solo pastor cannot support more than 150 people.
- Power shifts from the laity to the staff. Staff now know more about church members than the lay leaders often do. Lay leaders delegate and empower staff for day to day decisions.
- Churches are invited to be more intentional in communication and helping guests connect. It takes more than word of mouth for more friends to engage and participate.
- Lastly, the church must be willing for the pastor to lead more and shepherd less. This means the pastor is needed most in

vision casting, strategy, and administration. They are less
available and accessible. The church is cared for through
systems of pastoral care.

During our time in Marysville, I held these systemic truths in mind as
we navigated each area of our life together. From day one, I arranged
this church community so it could grow. But I wrestled with whether
or not the church wanted to grow. Was I forcing this on them? I
desperately wanted people to know they could belong and were loved
and could be free. All the while, a part of me resisted the very growth I
was making room for. It was very confusing.

As I got signals from church leaders that they were open to exploring,
we took one step at a time. As the church welcome more guests who
became active participants, grief rumbled around the edges. It didn't
look like grief though. It looked like complaints about change,
concern about something being moved, kindly worded emails about
how something had been done before. A sermon series about the gift
and growth of grief helped us put language to some of what we were
experiencing. We were happy to meet new friends and welcome them
into faith community. And the growth was tricky. So much was
changing. We worked hard to normalize the feelings and name our
new realities. Former Marysville pastor, Rev. Rody Rowe once asked,
"Do you get to know everyone or does everyone get to know Jesus?"
We asked that question a lot.

Loneliness

While the wider church body wrestled with their feelings about the
growth, I was doing the same. I missed getting to know everyone. I'll
never forget the day we stood up to lead our confirmation class
through a beautiful moment to publicly declare their faith in God. I
looked around and realized I didn't know these kids like I'd known
youth group kids in the past. As I laid my hands on their shoulders
and prayed, I didn't know their favorite movies or after school snacks.
As I named God in them, I didn't know their fears and challenges in

the hallways of their schools. This made me want to change all our jobs so I could be more present with the youth of our church on the spot. I felt left out. Isolated. Sad.

I also knew this was a sign our church was growing. Someone once said, "The leader is the lid to every organization." I believe it. If I couldn't let go of being involved in every area of our church, then my capacity to lead would diminish. So, as hard as it was, I went home that day and had a good cry. Then I sent a video message to our team and shared my joy due to their beautiful work to nurture and encourage our youth that year. I shared my pride in the team and gratitude at getting to be a part of it. I also shared with them something I was learning that day. That it was okay for me to feel left out. It didn't mean I wasn't doing my job. It meant I was doing my job well.

Disrupting the Status Quo

One reason I've apologized for growth comes from the denomination I was born into. Ever since my college and seminary days, the narrative of the United Methodist Church has been decline and death. We braced ourselves at leadership gatherings for the sobering statistics of decreasing attendance, fewer professions of faith, increasing signs that "church as it used to be" was rapidly disappearing. Growing up, I sensed pride in our core values of the Wesleyan and Methodist movements, but the overarching message was, "Our churches are dying." As people beat their heads against the wall looking for creative ways to reverse the decline, a very specific message hung in the air for new candidates for ministry. "Young clergy, save us."

It would have been helpful if my 21-year-old self was mature enough to set a boundary and not pick up that invitation. But I didn't know any better. I knew God was calling me to serve as a pastor in the United Methodist Church and that, apparently, all our churches needed saving. And not necessarily by Jesus, but by new pastors. Hmm. This could be a problem.

One day I named a new realization to Julia in a coaching call. "How do I grow with joy when I was born into fearful soil?" On one level, I lived inside anxiety like it was my job. I was afraid of growth because it would challenge the safe patterns I'd created. On another level, I lived inside the United Methodist Church, which was breathing the fear in the air in a real way.

It hit me. *I'm struggling to disrupt the status quo of the death narrative and truly help a church grow.* I didn't want people to judge and shame me for leading a healthy church. I've seen how colleagues judge the pastor at the "bigger church down the road." Pastors are human too and we're complicated people.

I was left with a growing church that I loved and yet felt wildly apologetic for. I struggled to celebrate the growth with our church. I purposely didn't talk about it outside a small circles of colleagues. Then one day, I realized maybe this was also about control.

Control & Fear

I said to Julia one day while pacing the sanctuary, "It feels like I've been holding the floodwaters back and I'm so tired of trying to control something that most of us don't want to control." Yes, learning how to relate to the growth of this faith community was also about control. While I taught others to open their clenched fists, mine were refusing to release outcomes.

Part of me didn't want to let go and celebrate because I'd feel overwhelmed by how much I wasn't in control of the goodness. If I can't make all these great things happen, then I'll realize again how vulnerable I am. As long as I don't pause to celebrate, I can fool myself into believing I'm in charge. My frenetic activity proves I'm needed. Necessary. Important.

If I let go, the whole thing would fall apart. It felt too good to be true. This can't be real. My ego jumped in, "You've fooled them all! They think you're good at this stuff." So I constantly doubted God's work in this faith community while holding a ridiculous heavy expectation that it all rested on me.

Expansion of Self & Preempting the System

One day I watched as Rachel Billups was named the new senior pastor of Ginghamsburg Church in Ohio. I burst into tears. Which was confusing. I'd been pushing away from the large church mentality and was on a kick of doing church in smaller communities. And yet, my tears were whispering something. *That's what it looks like when a woman takes up her space.*

God, my heart wanted that. Desperately. All this control and apology and resisting felt exhausting. Especially, when the church kept growing, regardless of how much I equally made room for it *and* tried to stop it.

The deeper shift came on a coaching call with Julia one November afternoon as I paced in the sanctuary while holding the phone to my ear. We talked about my hang-up around getting to year number five in an appointment. I was struggling with some big dreams and trying to fit them in my small box of what was allowed. Was it okay to move toward a bold new step if I didn't know how long they'd let me stay here? I named the ongoing reality of how difficult it is to dream when pastors are appointed one year at a time.

Julia curiously asked, "Jenny, what happens if you put a moratorium on doing the system's job of making yourself small before it does it for you?"

Was I pre-empting the system? I know how this is going to go. They're going to move me someday and it'll disrupt the fun big things we were working on here, so I might as well not do those things.

I was desperately trying to control the Holy Spirit. And in the end, I was the one suffering.

I pressed pause on my insane drive to do the "right" thing and finally whispered, "My heart wants to preach to thousands of people." I immediately backed into a dark corner of shame. Who says that kind of thing? Someone with a massive ego who thinks they're amazing, that's who.

Julia encouraged me to continue. I went on, "My heart wants to be big. It wants to take up my space. But the system keeps us small." I burst into tears. Between sniffles, I said, "It's not okay to want that. Women don't say that." Julia gently said on the other end of the line, "Yes, they do."

It was rather convenient when I could blame a system, a culture, old beliefs or my ego. Then it could be someone else's fault why I was resisting the expansion of myself in the world. Without my comfortable walls of fear to hide behind, I had no idea how to take up the space that was given to me to take up. As long as I could blame others and my ego and my fear, I didn't have to do the things burning in my heart.

But now? I'm seeing that this might be something else. I'm naming and claiming that God is the source of this energy, vision, and invitation. It's not my fear. The signs have been there all along. This gnawing sense that I was not fully embodying the space that was mine to share with the world. The whole time shame hissed me back into my box, preying on my fear of arrogance and ego.

I shook with emotion and courage and gratitude that day. *This is who I've been the whole time. The bigness is God. It's me. It's not something to be resisted and denied. Wow. I wonder what I'd say yes to if I let go again.*

So sure, it was about church growth.

And.

It was about reckoning with old stories about power, leadership, identity, gender, and courage. Here's to noticing the moments we shrink back in fear and refuse to take up our space. God hopes we'll sit with that for a second longer and let the story unravel to the ground.

Because God's dream is for each of us to fully expand and fill the glorious space given to us as a child of God.

Keep Celebrating

There's a moment between celebration
and moving to the next thing
that's vulnerable
naked
fragile

Why do we move on so quickly
from celebration?

We may fear it's all about us
so we deflect
change the conversation
praise someone else

Or maybe
we're afraid
that in celebrating the wildness
of joy
that we'll feel out of control

Is joy too slippery for us?
Is it too unpredictable?

So we let the big and small moments
in our life float past
while our eyes quickly scurry
to the next thing on our list

Today
may we choose
to pause and
sink in to celebration
to joy
to hard work
to energy shared
to time given
to partners
to change made

If we don't learn to celebrate
maybe the thing isn't actually complete

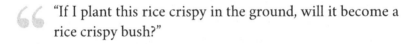

"If I plant this rice crispy in the ground, will it become a rice crispy bush?"

— Isabella

Why You Can't Wait Anymore for An Invitation to Lead Differently | December 8, 2018

Remember high school homecoming dance season? I recall nervously waiting for someone to ask me to what felt like the most important social gathering of my entire life. Fifteen-year-old girls don't skimp when it comes to high drama. We over-exaggerate with the best of them. My inner critic was on overdrive. "No one's going to ask you. The couple guys you think are cute are going to ask those other girls. Who are you to think someone wants to dance with you?"

Ouch.

When you're fifteen, you don't know those voices aren't true. Those voices keep you frozen. You stay small, hoping no one will notice you. You reel in your joy like a fish on the end of the line.

One year I decided this waiting, worry, and self-doubt was silly so I invited a friend. He said yes. We met at our high school gym the night of homecoming, we awkwardly danced and I rushed to the bathroom afterward to talk with my friends. We giggled and swapped stories of embarrassing moments.

It was not a night of overwhelming confidence and courage. It bubbled over with tentative uncomfortable nerves in only a way fifteen-year-old kids can know. But I learned something that night. You don't have to wait for an invitation to the party. This is a helpful reminder because lately I've been waiting for an invitation to a party I'm already at.

I love leadership. I love healthy, grounded, courageous, intentional leadership. A quick scan of my Instagram feed shows you I follow and listen to a lot of leaders who love those things. Most of them identify as female.

A quick scan around my real-life feed – the people I watch lead and facilitate in real life – mostly identify as male.

I've noticed this truth before but didn't think much of it. I knew who I was and would simply keep leading how I felt called to lead. But recently, something shifted.

There's some new work that my heart is inviting, nudging and shoving me toward. It feels like high school homecoming dance season all over again as I test that call and seek some clarity.

Despite my beloved inner critic working in overdrive, the invitation to speak into a space differently was growing stronger, and yet I was holding back. I saw myself looking for validation and permission to do this work. I was troubled by who I needed it from. One day, it hit me and I couldn't believe I didn't see it earlier.

I was literally waiting for permission from men to lead differently. This is a disturbing realization for a feminist-patriarchy-smashing woman who's had no problem saying yes to being a female leader in a previously male-dominated culture. It's a little embarrassing to see this stale belief rise to the surface. That in 2018, some of us feel like we still need permission from men to be who we were called to be. And yet, I'm not surprised. Because in 2018, we are pulling back the veil on sexism in a compelling way. It's painful to see what's underneath but if justice is our invitation then we must each do the work to identify old assumptions buried underneath years of status quo.

As life would have it, I was surrounded by female colleagues at the time of this realization. Their support, encouragement, affirmation, and deep "yes" was the invitation I was looking for. This was affirmed when I heard our female bishop speak and tears streamed down my cheeks. Watching her lead moves me in a profoundly deep way.

Is there a new adventure you're being invited into? Are you waiting for an invitation into that work when your heart already knows it's your work and this is the season?

Here's to saying yes to the wild invitations of our God. Here's to naming when we seek an invitation from someone who can't give it to us. And here's to taking the next step forward, even when it's uncomfortable.

Waiting For An Invitation

Are you waiting for an invitation
to a party that doesn't yet exist?

Your heart is relentless
Pointing wildly
to work that is yours to do

in this world

You see what is
You see what could be

Your heart is sending
a very clear invitation

But instead
you look everywhere else
for permission, affirmation,
encouragement, an invitation

There must be a secret committee
issuing invites to your work
in the world

Fear is whispering
Fear has a big dressing room
and loves to play dress up
Fear disguises itself as
insecurity
self-doubt
hesitation

The only invitation you need
is the one you already have

Your heart hand delivered
an invitation full of Vision
New possibility
A profound way of being

Don't expect others
to invite you to work

that will challenge and change
the norm

That invitation will likely
never come

Listen
Deeply
A voice is calling and saying
Yes
You're invited

Just Me

Do you know what's terrifying?
When your job goes from
getting tasks done
to being with people

We know how to do tasks
Put them on a list

Do them
Success!
Worth!
Value!
Productivity!

But what do you do
when the person becomes
more important than the task?

The deeper work calls
The vulnerability makes you shake
The fear wants the easier task
You can't hide behind tasks
anymore

But you can measure
Define and
Control tasks

Conversations are hard to measure
Define and
Control

People can't fit on a to do list
so it's time to face the truth
that if you want to make a
difference in our world
beyond tasks
you'll have to start
valuing something
that's hard to measure

And face the truth
that maybe all that's needed

is you.

Not your tasks, your effort,
your list or your control.
Just you.
It's terrifying, isn't it?
But it's worth it.

Your Palms Up Life | January 3, 2019

I've been dreaming about an email for a while. It's kind of a weird thing to dream about. But I wondered what might happen if I created a beautiful email and sent it to incredible people. Yeah, I know. Emails and beautiful are not two things I'd usually put together. Email often feels like a necessary evil to exist in our world today.

But what if an email could be beautiful?

What if two times a month, you opened up an email that left you feeling more at ease instead of pressured to move faster? More empowered and courageous rather than disconnected and fearful. Maybe an email could even clear the clutter around your heart so you could show up to your one holy life.

Welcome to Your Palms Up Life!

It's a twice a month email for spiritually-minded people who want to let go of overwhelm with courage and ease.

It's an invitation to pause, listen a little deeper, to ask a new question, hear a new perspective and emerge more grounded and focused on what matters most to you in this life.

Your time really matters to me. I promise not to waste it. You don't need another email that promises to fix everything or ten steps to happiness.

I'm guessing you might need what I need. A few trusted voices who have struggled and emerged on the other side with something compelling. They've seen something and they're trying to put it into words. They're grounded in something that feels stronger and meaningful.

I'm hoping and praying you find some of those voices here.

A Soft Letting Go

I saw a yellow tattered leaf today
fall from its home
Branch by branch by branch
it fell
The lowest branch
caught the leaf
It was such a soft and quiet
letting go
No drama, excitement or shout
The leaf simply fell
because it was time

It fell softly and gracefully
The leaf seemed to trust
the unfolding of things

What if our letting go was soft?
Could we let go of the things
not meant for us anymore?

No drama
No fear
No what if scenarios

Let the leaf fall softly
Listen to the sound of freedom

God is Ridiculous | March 28, 2019

God, how good are you?! Are you inviting me to write and gift something to others *and* you're giving me people to help lead in our community *and* challenging me with some of my hang-ups?! You are ridiculous. :)

 "How is it raining yesterday and today?"

— ISABELLA

Letting Go Takes Practice | April 2, 2019

Letting go takes practice. I was swimming laps recently at the Marysville YMCA and came to one of my favorite moves. The one where I swim on my back and float down the lane with pretty minimal kicking. If you saw me, you might think I was drowning or at least being pretty lazy. But in reality, this has become one of my spiritual practices.

Floating invites me to trust the thickness of the water. To give myself over to another force that supports my body. My ears go underwater and sound softens. I memorize how my body feels at that moment. I am supported by something else. My body lets go.

Fear Changed Clothes

I thought I knew fear
We've battled
Gone to war
We both have scars

Then we came to understand each other
We even shook hands one day

But then fear changed clothes

I didn't recognize the new look
Fear fooled me
Lulled me
Back into submission

I hate when fear changes clothes

An Easter Sermon About The Time I Flew to Oregon | April 21, 2019

A few months ago I got on a plane to go have a really hard conversation with someone who has loved me every single day of my life. My dad. A couple of months of therapy and digging deeper into some unhealthy areas in my life had shown me the things we pick up as children -- habits and beliefs and ways of being -- need closer examination at times. Sometimes our experiences in other seasons of our life come back to haunt us. Those ghosts dance around the edges of our lives at times, not wanting to take center stage. They prefer that spot just off stage where we can't quite name why they're scary and unpredictable, but we know they are there.

In therapy, I put more puzzle pieces together about how I grew up, about what I learned in our family system, and how I adapted. Very normal behavior for every single person on the planet. Our family's shape us. But at some point, those habits get ingrained and become our way of life without us realizing some of those habits aren't serving us well.

So I took a deep breath, bought a plane ticket, asked Kate to preach that Sunday and drove to the airport. I nervously sat through the plane ride, reminding myself to release the outcome over and over and over and over. In the deepest part of myself, I knew everything would be fine. But my body was not on the same page.

I arrived. Dinner time approached and I hopped into my Dad's truck to go to a restaurant. By the time we got to the first stop sign, I said, "So there are some things I was hoping we could talk about tonight. Things I'm learning from working on myself." He replied, "Uh oh..." I quickly said, "We don't have to. I want it to be something you want to hear and process a bit." He said, "Sure, why don't you start now?" So I took a deep breath and started talking. We show up scared, right?

As we engage with the story of Easter, one sentence rose above the rest for me this year. "Why do you look for the living among the dead?" Two men in gleaming bright clothing (indicating power from God) surprise the women with this question. Let us remember the women were grieving for Jesus. They went to the tomb as Sabbath ended so they could get to work preparing his body for burial. You know how we keep ourselves busy when life gets hard? It gives us something to focus on besides the awful thing that's ripping our hearts in two. Yeah, the women of Easter morning know that feeling too.

But their busy work and preparation were shockingly interrupted. "Why do you look for the living among the dead?"

If I was there, I would have gazed up at one of these guys and said, "We're not looking for the living. We're loving the person who died."

In this exchange, I see truth for many of us. Sometimes we settle for preparing the spices and burying the dead. We want to be fully alive in this one life we get. But we don't know how that might happen. So we care for what's in front of us. And sometimes we get stuck with what's in front of us. We adjust to life after loss. As the losses pile up, our job is to figure out how to just get through it. Yes, there's a time for survival mode. It's called shock and it's a normal human response. But some of us have lived in survival mode for so long that it's all we know.

The Jesus who woke up and walked out of a dark tomb wants to save us from wandering around our dark tombs, living in survival mode. Those men in gleaming light said to the women and they say to us, "He's not here."

For anyone who feels like they've been stuck in survival mode for far too long, Jesus wants to ridiculously interrupt this way of being. Jesus sees our survival mode. He doesn't judge it. He doesn't criticize it. Jesus gently smiles, "Why do you look for the living among the dead?"

Back to that conversation with my dad. It turns out when you summon enough courage and you're willing to show up scared, new life gets room to stretch and come alive.

For the next hour or two, everything tumbled out of me, in a restaurant in Oregon. All the things I had come to believe were true. Just because of how I coped with life at six years old. And here I am at 36, still believing some of them are true. There were tears from both of us, a little confusion from our waitress at what was going on and so much life bursting forth as we both let down the protective walls we built to keep people from hurting us. I felt alive.

All these heavy things I'd been holding for decades vanished. I felt light and free.

Then as we were wrapping up, I said, "It goes without saying, but Dad, I forgive you." He grabbed my hand, with a tight jaw full of emotion, and looked me right in the eyes. I continued, "Dad, I forgive you for any pain and heartache you caused me when I was growing up." His eyes glistened with tears. Tears streamed down my cheeks. "Thank you," he said.

Freedom.

I moved from death to life.

You're invited to the same journey in your own way. We're invited to the same movement in our collective life together.

As we invite the Easter story to teach us about moving from death to life today, here are a few things to think about.

Moving from death to life is creative.

Resurrection is inherently creative. We're invited to see what can't be seen yet. We're the women in the empty tomb taking care of something we lost. We don't see the new thing yet. Life is more than survival mode in our dark tombs. Moving from death to life means we don't have to keep looking at life the same way we are right now. We don't have to spin around our lives cluttered with old beliefs, stuck perspectives, and tired pain looking for a way out through only what we see. We get to reimagine. Easter can give us a new vision of what's possible.

Moving from death to life is often slow.

It's ironic to point out what happens in Luke 24:11 CEB: *Their words struck the apostles as nonsense, and they didn't believe the women.* The men who spent the most time with Jesus didn't believe he was alive. The women who also spent as much time with Jesus are the first to witness and to share the good news. Our God continues to have deep compassion and love for anyone who is pushed to the margins. And the ways we move from death to life are often slow. Sometimes we get it. Sometimes we don't. We want the quick fix, the pill, the strategy, and the steps. If you want a strategy from God, it's love people. Which is not usually a quick process. This work we're all a part of, friends, it is slow work. But it's good work.

Moving from death to life is God's dream for us as a worldwide community.

We want to live in the overflow of each person fully alive. What does this mean for our collective life together? It means we do the work to pause and ask ourselves how we each continue to be complicit in benefitting from systems that give life to some and death to others. If we are to be Easter people, people of the resurrection, then we consider how we treat women, men, children, members of the LGBTQ community, people of a different race and ethnicity than you, someone who votes differently than you. We question our relationship to money as a community, to our planet, to our resources, to immigrants. How do we continue cycles of violence?

Easter invites us to take a hard look in the mirror and see how we contribute to the very systems that got Jesus killed. Sometimes it's easier to point out those who denied Jesus instead of owning the truth that if we were there, we might have faded into the crowd as well. God's dream is for us all to move from death to life.

"Why do you look for the living among the dead?"

Today, our friend, Lisa is getting baptized! I invited her to share with you: "I first was introduced to Marysville United Methodist Church about three and a half years ago because I had a fine to pay with community service. I called Kloz 4 Kidz (K4K) and found myself talking with Linda Max. Within minutes Linda had me signed up to work in the portable the very same week.

After working with Linda a couple of times she started inviting me to come to church. I had no idea how much that invite, and K4K would change the direction of my life and fill a huge void that I always knew I had but wasn't sure how to fill. Needless to say I fell in love with K4K and this church.

I am going through some big life changes now, and it just feels so right to be "all in" as you put it. I am finally starting to feel at peace with who I am and I owe that to God #1 but the people of this church come in on a close second."

Lisa is moving from death to life.

Friends, long ago, followers of Jesus were asked, "why do you look for the living among the dead?" We're asked the same thing today. May we be Easter people. Sons and daughters of the resurrection who are willing to show up scared and enter into the difficult realities of our world because we know Love wants to live there too. Christ is risen! He is risen indeed. Amen.

Me: "Wesley, when you finish the game, let's put the iPad away."

Wesley: "Mom, I never finish this game. It goes on forever."

Practicing the Party | May 12, 2019

The other day I had an uncomfortable wake up call to what's really important in life. My six-year-old daughter found out we had an entire Saturday with no family commitments. "We get to stay home ALL day?!" My husband and I had a growing list of things we wanted to get done around the house. She just wanted to party. Literally.

Saturday morning, she came downstairs with a stuffed animal and blanket under one arm and a list in the other hand. In her mind, this wide open gift of a day would be filled with a PJ party, a dance party, crazy hats, decorations, balloons, cookies, milk and reading books.

I wasn't quite sure what to do. I noticed the conversation in my head: "She's sweet but doesn't understand there are other things that have to get done. Maybe I can convince her to have a party for about an hour after lunch."

She understood that her dad and I did have to do a couple of things so she and her younger brother danced around and blew up balloons. I went off to tackle my growing list of things I just had to do. But I noticed the pull back to the room the kids were in. A song would come on and I had to dance. A streamer would fall so I helped tape it back up. Her energy was contagious.

I felt oddly frustrated. This six-year-old was interrupting my productivity with her party. But this party felt more important than anything on my sacred to-do list. So I practiced celebration while dancing to the Trolls movie soundtrack in our kitchen. I cultivated joy while swinging my son around and hearing him giggle. I released stress from a busy week by watching them put together a gingerbread house.

Our celebration was disrupting my productivity. I needed this party. Maybe you do too.

Where The Waters Meet

There is a place where one set of waves meet another
You would think they would crash into each other
with their own momentum and route and movement
But they don't
Instead, the peaceful energy of one wave
mixes with the opposing energy of the other

No violence
No clashing
No selfishness
No force

Just ease

Each wave melts into the other with serene comfort

At this moment where the waters meet there is absolute peace
Acceptance of opposing realities
A compromising to each other
as a new path emerges
that only could appear
when two rival energies meet
and become something new

There is a place where the waters meet
If only our world would take note
of a different way to engage conflicting energies

What if the thing so adamantly opposed
Contains part of the new path forward?

Is it possible the two opposing energies
could truly meet
In non-violence
In grace
In love

And listen to each other?
This is where the waters meet

 "Don't put on the song yet. I can't dance and brush my teeth at the same time!"

— ISABELLA

JENNY SMITH

Stay in Your Lane

Stay in your lane
I hear whispered
in my general direction

They caught me again
Glancing over
at the other

Comparing
Contrasting
Judging
Proving
that my lane was better
That I would win
That I was enough

Until I got to the end of the lane
and saw the other next to me
was me

Racing myself
feels fun at first
Inviting
Exhilarating
Challenging

But after a while
it becomes painfully clear
that I won't get anywhere in this race

It's a waste of time
Gifts
Passion

Energy

The voice whispers again
Stay in your lane
I gave you the lane
To enjoy, create, love, give

Then one day maybe I'll realize
It was never a race in the first place

11

ALLOW AND ENJOY

Email | July 11, 2019

"You want me to answer my emails."

Bishop Elaine Stanovsky read this statement aloud at the end of Oregon-Idaho's Annual Conference gathering a few weeks ago. Participants had a previous opportunity to leave her notes with questions or concerns during the conference. There was a smattering of laughter and then she responded.

"I want you to know when I opened my email this morning, I had 89 new messages since last night. I want to answer your emails. And I want to answer the physical mail that you send me. And I know every week that things fall through the cracks. *And I know that the solution to our dilemma is not going to be that the Bishop works harder.*"

Cue tentative and confused applause from attendees.

She continued, "That's a confession. I give you my heart and I give you way more of my life than I should, honestly…I don't think we have a model that works for bishops in three conferences over four states with 440 churches. I'm doing my best but I'm not going to quit disappointing."

Some may have thought it a mundane exchange between a frustrated constituent and their leader. But it was far more than that.

"The answer is not for me to work harder."

This is a culture shift in one sentence.

This is sacred resistance.

This is a refusal to let a broken and ineffective system call the shots.

This is holy.

The answer is not for me to work harder.

What happens if an exhausted parent whispers this?

A burned-out executive? A stressed-out student?

When something is overwhelming and the work is piling up, our first inclination is to double down. We push up our sleeves and try harder. We summon a new wave of focused grit so we can power through the obstacle in front of us. Sometimes, that's the best answer. But more often, it's not.

What if you're being invited to bring the entire unsustainable culture to a screeching halt? You can do that, by the way.

You have permission to question it all.

Why do we do this?

How did it get like this?

Could this be different?

The answer is not for me to work harder.

When we cooperate with God, instead of our hustle culture, God can do far more in, through, and despite us. May we not give our lives to maintaining unhealthy, unjust, and broken ways of being because "that's just how it is."

It doesn't have to be that way. I wish you the courage to question the cultures you move in. May you show up scared. Even if your voice wobbles and your knees shake. Ask the questions rumbling in your being.

Freedom is waiting. Love hopes you'll speak.

 "Did Jesus have two dads? Joseph and God?"

— WESLEY

Enjoy the Joy

I would like to learn how to celebrate
Truly celebrate

It's easy to get so caught up
in the destination
that I hardly stop to notice
how far I've traveled

So today I choose
to sink in deep to joy
to give my spirit permission
to smile

Today I dance
Sing
Laugh

Cheer
and witness joy's persistence
in the face of distraction

I let go of the chase
and sink deep into joy
Into celebration
Into freedom

Today, I rest in joy
and allow myself to sustain celebration
instead of checking a list
and earning my worth
and moving on

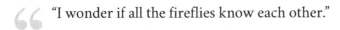

"I wonder if all the fireflies know each other."

— Isabella

Hidden in Plain Sight | December 6, 2019

During one of these long snow days we had recently, I asked my kids what they wanted to do. Isabella, our seven-year-old announced, "Let's play tag!" I started counting, they squealed and ran away.

I found them in short order and we played again. When it was Wesley's turn to count, I ran to the playroom and hid behind a very thin gray curtain. I stood behind the curtain and didn't move. I figured this hiding spot wouldn't last twenty seconds.

Much to my surprise, he ran past me once. Twice. Three times. He found his sister and she skipped into the playroom and sat down near me. I whispered and she laughed when she saw me. She told her brother in her sing-song voice, "Mom's in here, but I'm not telling you where."

He continued to look everywhere for me! I was so sure he could see me. After a good ten minutes, he finally lifted the curtain and saw his mom. A big grin spread across his little face, "I found you, Mom!"

I had a great ten minutes to stand there with my face pressed up against a very cold window with snow on the other side of it. There was some time to think and here's what I noticed. It's not rocket science, but I needed the reminder. Maybe you do too.

So much of what we look for is hidden in plain sight. Love, grace, forgiveness, wisdom, purpose, patience, new perspective, friendship, clarity, peace, joy, rest, understanding.

It's here. All around us. But we keep looking everywhere else for it.

The Work of Allowing

There is something in you
that wants to come out to play
I have a feeling you've
heard the whispers

You've seen glimpses of this thing
that's meant to be on the outside of you
Not stuck in the corner of your cramped heart
Patiently asleep
Waiting for the alarm, the news,
The text alert that it's finally time
to stretch
Blink open its eyes
To yawn

And wake up

Like a three-year-old
anxiously awaiting
recess time at preschool
Your thing
Your calling
Your work in the world
is beside itself with excitement
to be born through you

If you sense it's time
then your work of allowing begins

Allow what's already inside to
Come
Out
And
Play

Letting Go | January 16, 2020

I recently had an opportunity to travel for work and it was time to say goodbye to my daughter. I was to leave early the next morning so this was a bedtime goodbye. I quickly realized this would not go well. She was upset, anxious, and beside herself.

"Mama, can't another pastor go? Why do you have to go?"

We talked it out. The anxiety. The fear it gives us. We acknowledged her feelings. I smoothed her hair and rubbed her back.

It was time to stand up and leave her room. She wrapped those little arms around my neck and tearfully said, "Mama, don't go. Stay here. I'm never letting go."

Oh, dear.

 "Is there an oven here at Dairy Queen? I need to warm up this ice cream."

— WESLEY

You Can Question

What have you accepted as fact
that might not be fact?
What would happen if you questioned it?

What if the facts of your life are simply stories
you have chosen to see as true?

That means they could change
Become new

What would happen if you questioned
the stories about

Fear
A relationship
What you see in the mirror
What you think in the dark
Shame
Your childhood

What your parents told you
When you lost
Your job
A child
A grandchild
Losing a loved one
Death
Starting over

There's a chance that the story you're telling yourself
about these things
isn't true
anymore

Maybe it is.

But what if it's not?

I'm A Pastor, Not A Producer | March 22, 2020

I've wanted to quit online worship the last few Sundays since quarantine began. This is a surprise to me because we've been live streaming for four and a half years. I'm used to seeing my face on a screen. I'm used to my tech team reminding me (again) to stay inside the box of tape on the floor. I'm used to being asked which service felt like the best sermon so they could edit it for sharing later that day. This is why my desire to quit all this the last couple of weeks is surprising.

Sure, there are nuanced layers of grief mixed in. There's a chance I won't see my church family again before moving to a new appointment in June. I'm trying to figure out how to grieve and celebrate our time together without being able to see them. There's a whole set of emotions to navigate in living through a pandemic.

But the feeling I have after worship is a different kind of something not good.

It started when we moved our online streaming set up to our parsonage instead of the empty sanctuary where we'd been for the last three weeks. When in the sanctuary, sure it felt odd to talk only to a camera, but that was a fun challenge. I still had the muscle memory of leading worship from the same spot on the floor, with the chairs where they should be, with the tech booth where it always is, with light streaming in through the windows.

Now we're at home in a small office with five monitors, five computers, tablets, phones, tripods, microphones, a makeshift altar, instruments and cables. Our five and eight-year-olds are in the next room over coloring and crafting because we turned their tablets on airplane mode so they wouldn't crash our WiFi.

As someone who has been comfortable with social media for a long time and who gets the value of technology as a means to the grace of God, why am I struggling with this?

I feel like a producer, not a pastor.

My producer husband reminds me this is what our tech team has been doing for years. They're used to catching a glitch and muting a microphone. To holding in their breath when a feed drops for a moment. To getting a text from someone who can't hear from home.

I am not.

I'm used to doing my work to facilitate a gathering of the beloved community. As a pastor. The thing I'm trained and called to do. To pray, speak, encourage, comfort, challenge, and laugh.

I am not a producer.

And yet, here we are. Lots of us. Pastors who are now producers, to some degree.

The one thing that's kept me from quitting each week is a well-timed text from a church member sharing how much the service meant to them. *Thank you, Pastor. This meant a lot to me. I feel less alone. It's so good to gather this way.*

I take a deep breath. I remember how much I love these people. And I commit to try again next week.

I'm reminded that, in God's world, it's almost always "yes/and," not "either/or." Instead of being a producer or a pastor, *what does it look like to be a pastor in the midst of producing?*

It doesn't feel comfortable yet. I hope one day that it does. It's worth it for text messages from a friend like this: I am blessed because you risk this.

I see you, leaders. Let's keep risking this together. We'll keep showing up in new ways and spaces and formats and technologies if it means God gets a little more room to do what God loves to do.

All ways of being are up for discussion in this season. Here's to the changing of our identities as we adapt, innovate, cooperate, and release. God is inviting us forward.

Mic check. Mic check. One, two, three.

Wild Over Right

There's an energy inside
that's wild and free
My soul loves this energy
and controls it at the same time

This wild thing is unpredictable
Indefinable
Blurry

The wild is out of control

The wild doesn't have a manual
Best practices
Steps to follow

The wild is bigger than me
Stronger than me
Not dependent on me

Which makes the wild
Difficult
Uncomfortable
Scary

It's easier to just do what others think is right
What you think is right
Follow the spoken and unspoken rules

But every shift requires a holy question

What if the wild energy is a gift for this world
instead of a fearful thing to be
managed
bossed around
looked down on

Could the energy
come out to play?

Could wild bring joy on its wings
in a way right never could?

Dual Roles | April 2, 2020

Can pastors be friends with their church members? Lots of ink has been spilled over the complex issues surrounding this question. They talk about issues around boundaries, roles, power, and confidentiality. My dad, a retired pastor, and I have spoken about this many times. For more than a decade now, I've pushed back against common wisdom and said, "Yes, pastors can be friends with their church members." And it's one thing when you're an associate pastor. In Marysville, this was my first chance to sort out the reality of this belief on the ground as a lead pastor. Could I be friends with people I was also pastoring? Could I be friends with people on my staff team that I supervise?

Five years later, my verdict is yes and no. Yes, I can laugh, cry, listen, go out to dinner and share part of myself with beloved members in our church family. We can feel close and have a connection that certainly feels like friendship. But there are landmines everywhere. I am not allowed to offer my full self because I have a position of power. It's near impossible to nurture close friendships with people on my staff and then enter in a tough supervisory conversation the next day. I've spent five years trying to prove that wrong. But as I prepare for my next place of service, I think I've finally come to understand the truth of what so many in the business world understand.

The problem with church culture is that we expect everyone to be nice, comforting, and encouraging. And hopefully, people are practicing those beautiful truths of a Jesus community. But everyone in these beautiful Jesus communities is human. Which means they're also prideful, angry, mean, or rude at times.

We then extend those same expectations to our church staff space. Do we allow our pastor, who is expected to be gracious, calm, and understanding, to also be a tough supervisor when needed? Can we handle this person in a dual role? To complicate the matter further, most of our pastors have not had supervisory training. So we take humans called by God to nurture hearts and give them a list of employees to do goal setting, accountability, and supervision. Then we're surprised when the pastor struggles to know the difference between pastoring and supervising. There are days I now believe that once someone says yes to a staff position, the pastor can no longer be their pastor. The lines are too blurry.

Even while surrounded by incredible people in these five years, I felt lonely. I'm told this is normal for any senior leader in an organization. There are many roles to manage and it's near impossible to share your full self with anyone. We want to feel seen and heard. Known. When you have to do a mental dance with each person to remember the correct role in the moment, it's tricky for someone who deeply values transparency and vulnerability. It's my filter for everything. I have struggled, and appreciated, the opportunity in Marysville to explore the nuances of dual roles.

I hope that even in the midst of navigating role changes in milliseconds, I've been as present as possible to our staff, our leaders, our church members, and our community.

I'm thankful for the countless cups of hot chocolate I've shared with so many people in the past five years at Marysville. I count you as friends, even if it's a different kind of friendship. I think I'm finally okay with that. It's up to me to nurture friendships outside the church family where I get to be Jenny, not Pastor Jenny. And somehow, in the complication of it all, grace is here. Pastors need to hear this. Because it's often difficult to remember we're humans too. We hope people will see the full us and still want to hang out. We hope a few close friends will see our painful flaws and blind spots and accept us anyway. We often don't know what to do next in a tough situation and we long for people to give us grace too.

Here's to the dual roles and all the complicated ways we show up to and for each other. God makes it beautiful.

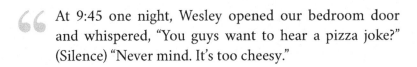

At 9:45 one night, Wesley opened our bedroom door and whispered, "You guys want to hear a pizza joke?" (Silence) "Never mind. It's too cheesy."

A Perfectionist's Prayer

God, I see you coming
to love me
comfort me
challenge me

But first, give me a minute,
I must clean up
all these things about me
that I don't like

My home needs to be clean
before you arrive

Plus, I'm sure there are things
I haven't realized
or can't see
or am denying
that I should fix
before you arrive

Just to be sure
that I deserve your love
your grace
your attention

Because surely you wouldn't
want to visit me

in my mess

Give me a minute
while I grab my broom

Seriously, God

This business about you working
in my weakness
is ridiculous

It's Okay to Make Mistakes | April 24, 2020

Every school day since preschool, I've said a little blessing with my daughter before we part ways for our adventures in the world. As we pulled up, first to daycare and now to elementary school, I would say these words, "Today I hope you have fun, you play hard, you're safe, you learn something new, you know it's okay to make mistakes and you show people they are loved! Amen."

She would say a few of the words with me. One day, when she was around three years old, she said "mis-nakes" instead of "mistakes." She giggled incessantly and continued to say "misnakes" for years to come.

She said it a few months ago and she's eight.

It's okay to make misnakes.

So Much Freaking Room

My life feels like a train station

It used to be full of people
Going every which way
Hurrying to unknown destinations
Agendas to follow
Plans to execute
Not always sure why or
where they were going

But they were going

Then one day I woke up
and realized the energy
that relentlessly kept
buying train tickets
was tired
worn out
exhausted
and ready to let go

The old energy and I
had one last warm drink together
and said goodbye

Now my life feels like
an empty train station

I stand in the middle
Just me
My heart
And my body
With arms outstretched

Ready to receive a new life

My strong voice echoes
The silence is light and comfortable
The busy click of shoes is replaced with
Quiet
Clarity
Peace
Room

There's so much freaking room
inside my life now that the
old energy said goodbye

I walk around the empty train station
and slowly
Intentionally
Mindfully

Choose one ticket on one train
headed to the next place
I want to go

But this time joy leads the way

12

LEADERSHIP MATTERS

Coaching with Julia | 2017-2020

I meandered down our dark preschool hallway with my phone tucked between my ear and my shoulder. I heard Julia's voice and imagined what she might look like. I couldn't quite put together a picture in my head but I knew right away what her voice felt like. Safety. Support. Honesty. Encouragement. I breathed a deep sigh and felt gratitude rise for this woman and the gift she was about to give me.

A few weeks earlier, I had asked my District Superintendent for a coaching referral. I was about ten months into the Marysville appointment and I was increasingly aware of how much I didn't know about what might be ahead. Not one to sit back and wait, I jumped at the chance to get a coach. My District Superintendent mentioned Julia. We spoke on the phone that day, both sizing each other up. Was this a person I wanted to invest in? Yes. So I filled out the paperwork, scheduled the first couple sessions, and off we went!

And now, four years later, we still meet via phone twice a month for coaching. I call her, she greets me and asks how I'm doing and where

I'm stuck. For fifty minutes, I tell her all kinds of stories, ask questions, and wonder aloud. She never gives me the answer I want to fix a difficult situation. But she asks just the right questions that shifts my perspective.

Whenever someone shares their joy at the interesting things unfolding in Marysville, I tell people about Julia. "She's one of the reasons we've been able to move forward in the past couple years. What would usually take me several months to figure out on my own, gets unstuck with her in fifty minutes." I encourage my colleagues to look into getting a coach. Use that professional expense account. It's worth every single penny. Our churches benefit, our sanity is maintained and the beloved community of God is strengthened.

As my dad always says, "Leadership is about asking great questions." Julia is one of the best. Here are some of our favorite questions and learnings together in our coaching relationship so far…

What would burning the book of best practices look like? There is no road map for what I'm experiencing. I'm trying to tape together road maps from other places. They won't send me where I want to go.

Whatever takes me toward liberation is where I have to go.

I don't believe failure is possible anymore. The cushion of grace around me feels secure.

"I don't know what I'm doing." This is a story I keep telling myself. It's a lie. It's a preemptive strike so others won't catch me being imperfect.

The movement of the Spirit may not have a book of best practices.

What's mine to do today?

What work habits did I create while in the mindset of fear that now don't serve me?

Your groundedness is a gift to everyone who comes in contact with your community.

How can I increase my capacity for enjoying this season?

Maybe the thing I help incarnate in them isn't the outcome or product but the hunger for it.

What am I afraid of when I invite people into something new?

I am in a season of pruning. I get to decide what I breathe life back into.

What kind of person do I want to be as I do this work?

How does my energy affect people?

The things that have been traps are becoming tools. I'm spending so much time getting to know the trap that now I can use it on purpose for good.

Do people know what I expect of them? Am I clear?

My people can't go where I haven't been willing to go. What's the step ahead of where they might be going that I can experience now?

I'm handing people a good thing that won't be easy at first.

In a stable system, I'm pulling a thread that will introduce instability at first. I have to pull the thread. It's what a leader does. I also want to own the grief that I'm now the string-puller. I will introduce anxiety in to my community. What else can I call it besides anxiety? I'm inviting people into liminal space on purpose. It feels like anxiety, but it's really about transformation.

The failing is in the not following.

The process is the point. How we walk across the bridge is more important than where we end up.

I had underestimated how much my people would grow through this process.

How will I make sure I'm holding this lightly enough that it can breathe?

I'll never know the whole plan. I sense that I could enjoy settling into not knowing. There is no road map at all. I could end up loving this.

When I feel the tightness or fatigue, it's my body whispering, "I'm trying to catch up. Wait for me."

What do you do when the long, slow, miraculous work of God feels boring?

For people with high self-expectations, how does gentleness fit in?

What if my body moves at the pace of my people? What is it at the right pace for? It's at the right pace to listen to Spirit.

Do not skip reflection time following a big action. It must be a key season of everything we do. Or I'll always feel this way. Right after a baby, we don't have another new one right away. We need to slow down and listen to what's next for us. What's the rush? This is how we operate. We do hard things that take a long time. We persist.

Sabbath question: Will it make me more of myself (feed the core of me) or will it feed my personality (get stuff done)?

What are the secret rules I still believe are true?

Part of me doesn't want to celebrate because I'll be overwhelmed by how much I'm not in control of the goodness. If I can't make all these great things happen, then I'll realize again how vulnerable I am. As long as I don't pause to celebrate, I can fool myself into believing I'm in charge. My frenetic activity proves I'm needed. And necessary. And important.

I'm so afraid I'll accidentally take credit that I don't even give God the gratitude.

What would it look like to build in a culture of celebration in our

faith community? **Celebration feels like doing less. It looks a lot like Sabbath.**

A pause is not an ending. It's movement. Pausing doesn't mean losing momentum. A pause moves us to a new place. Now we're refreshed.

Evil would love for me to not celebrate. Because then shame and guilt and scarcity win. Rest, wonder and celebration interrupt that power.

My fear of celebration steals the joy from other people.

Who am I to do this?

What does it mean to be a writer who pastors?

What does it mean to be a pastor who writes?

What if I started practicing the wild thing instead of the right thing?

Everyone wins when the leader gets quiet.

How can I use this anger well?

It feels like things are flowing through me but not exhausting me.

If I don't visit grief, it will visit me back.

I'm grieving that my leadership style has to change yet again. Leading this place is asking so much of me. Shedding the layers of what is comfortable and known. It's difficult and very uncomfortable.

What else do I need to let go of so I can steward what God is offering?

There's no formula. We learn by doing. There's no failure.

The stretch for me is to not miss this while it's happening because I'm thinking about what's next. It exists because it exists. Not because of what it will produce. If it's good, it will replicate. It's good enough, whether it recreates itself or not.

In helping our church community grow, I handed off responsibili-

ties to others so it could multiply. This is good. But I also miss feeling close to so many people. There's grief in this.

I can hold the vision and share it without doing all the heavy lifting.

Thriver's guilt is a thing.

What information do I think my team has that they, in reality, haven't gotten?

How do you grow with joy when you were born into fearful soil?

It feels like my inner critic has lost its edge. Praise Jesus.

Single Board Transition | 2016-2020

I remember getting a tour of the church in February 2015 with Kim and Kass. We paused outside the church library and I asked what the administrative structure was like. They rattled off the typical list of committees and how it felt like there was a meeting every week. I sensed their joy in participating and something else. Was it tiredness? Obligation? I didn't know yet but I felt it in my bones. Even then, I wondered what a sustainable leadership structure could be. I stood there talking to them while holding a five-month-old baby and wondering how in the world I could do this mom and lead pastor thing at the same time. I took a deep breath and followed them down the preschool hallway to see Isabella's future classroom. I pushed away the fear.

I loved getting to know our Administrative Council, Staff Parish Relations, Trustees & Finance Teams in my first months at the church. They were full of passionate people who adored this faith community. Again that sense of fatigue settled in my spirit as I heard what they said and didn't say. I filed it away as we learned how to work together for our common mission. Each church I served in the past used a traditional administrative structure with multiple committees so I didn't know anything else was possible. As in other churches, I noticed the tendency toward reporting ministry instead of visioning for the future. I wondered what structure would enable us to dream about what could be alongside sharing what was happening now. Maybe a separate team would be the answer.

In February, I invited our Administrative Council to meet in the sanctuary instead of the fellowship hall where we typically met. We set up chairs in a circle. We lit a candle together and I shared my desire to do more vision work. I shared my love for this community and the deep belief that God could do some incredible things through the people of Marysville United Methodist Church. We wondered aloud what that could look like.

A couple of months later, someone mentioned Stephan Ross's book, "Leadership for Fruitful Congregations." It describes a single board governance model that many churches considered a solution to several issues. It was becoming more difficult to fill the number of committee positions that are mandated by the Book of Discipline for our current structure. Decisions were taking too long to move through our committee structure. We were stuck in reporting mode instead of vision, setting goals and productive policy work.

Our existing Administrative Council chair invited those interested to read Ross's book. We gathered in a smaller group throughout the summer and wondered together if this model would serve our church moving forward. It's a single board that consists of sub-teams for Staff Parish Relations, Trustees, Finance, and Lay Leadership. It separates the policy development and governance from the day to day operations of the church, which move to staff.

One of my favorite outcomes of this conversation was getting to visit most groups in the church to have one specific conversation. Ross believes there are three types of leadership folks in a church. First, some love meetings. They love getting to talk and dream and get curious about the future. Second, some people love to be a part of a team. Give them a problem to solve and a few people to help and they're fully alive. Third, some people love direct hands-on ministry. Give them clothes to fold with Kloz 4 Kids and they're happy as can be.

In each group, we invited folks to identify which one or two of those descriptions best fit them. We took turns guessing what other people in the group might be as well. It led to the one conversation I had across most groups in the church family: It's okay to stop serving in a place you don't love anymore. It's okay to take a break. It's okay to move into a space you love.

That one conversation unlocked incredible energy in this church family. That weight, that exhaustion, that sense of duty had been real. The energy felt heavy. But in the months to come, the energy shifted. People who'd been exhausted but didn't feel like they could step away, did. I received many emails and phone calls from people ready to hang up their hats for a while. I welcomed every single one with grace, understanding and affirmation. It wasn't failure or dropping the ball. It was fear that no one would pick up the thing they loved. It was frustration that life was changing and they were done, but didn't know how to step away. Given the permission, it felt like the Spirit rippled out from the center in joyful ways.

Meanwhile, the incredibly brave church leaders talked to everyone about this new single board structure. Could this serve us well for the next season? What are our concerns with it? We brought Stephan Ross to lead a workshop so everyone could get their questions out on the table. Sensing mostly positive energy around this new idea, we continued to pray and plan and discern new leaders for this structure. We met for multiple town hall conversations where everyone could weigh in.

We arrived at a charge conference with our District Superintendent. The vote came. Results were tallied. It passed by 99%. We invited our new leaders for what we called our Vision Team to stand. Prayers were lifted and the new structure officially began January 1, 2017.

Ever since, I've met with pastors and leaders who are considering this model. They always ask me how it's going now. And here's what I say…

First, we only got this off the ground because of God and Anne Rodeheaver. Anne specializes in change management and she was the perfect person to serve as our first Vision Team chair when we needed the most structural help.

Second, it's still a work in progress. We tried to be honest with the church about that. Changing communication pathways, authority roles, and confidentiality rhythms for a faith community of this size takes effort on everyone's part. It's not easy.

Third, we were intentional with the people who served on our Vision Team. Our Leadership Development Team was responsible for looking around the church and prayerfully inviting people to serve who specifically had a passion for governance and visioning. We were careful not to invite people who would rather be serving at Community Lunch on Mondays. They simply wouldn't enjoy four-hour meetings on five Saturdays a year. Having the permission and freedom to discern and invite based on skillset and passion, instead of a warm body to fill a needed spot changed everything.

Fourth, a single board structure has enabled us to move on a dime. When a problem presented itself, we had the experts in Finance, Trustees, and Staff-Parish all together in the same room. Instead of moving a topic through monthly meetings across three committees (which all wanted the pastor's presence), a well-researched issue was brought before all those groups in the same meeting. I watched our leaders make wise, efficient, and effective decisions because they each had a better working knowledge of other sub-groups. The collaboration and partnership was incredible to watch.

Fifth, this structure birthed bigger visions than we ever could have moved forward in our former structure. I'll never forget bringing the beginning of the 10 in 30 vision to this group. They took a deep breath, leaned in, asked a million questions, and took a risk. We borrowed each other's bold belief and kept wondering what God could do in and through us.

That's the story of how the single board governance model became reality at Marysville United Methodist Church. It was far from perfect, but it was our best attempt in this season to respond to God's invitation to show up to our wider community. We hope it brought more joy, life, and freedom to our church members as they served and led in ways that lined up with their gifts. We hope more grace and love emerged in Marysville because of our willingness to let go of ways of being that served us in the past. We hope we more effectively served others and welcomed Christ because of this change.

Thank you to every single member of our Vision Team from 2017-2020: Anne, Jeff, Betsy, Dave M., Ken, Mel, Briannan, Donna, Gail, Darrell, Paula, Barb, Tom, Don, Chris, Dave R., Sue, Melinda, Amy, Scott, Vern, Lisa, Lauren, Rob, Sherry, Ken, Paul and Pastor Tanya.

The work we did together mattered.

The devotionals and conversation centered us in God's Spirit.

The hosting in our homes deepened our relationships.

The retreat meetings gave us time to dig in deep to big questions.

The trust in each other's perspectives and wisdom was astounding.

The way you risked and tried something new is a gift that honors God.

The way you supported and cheered me on is forever imprinted on my heart.

I could not have asked for a more incredible learning and growth opportunity in leadership in the local church. Thank you, beloved friends. It was an honor.

Palms Up Leadership Cohort | 2019-2020

People love to put pastors up on pedestals, as if they are superhuman. Closer to God. Saints.

We are not.

I hate to break your heart, in case this is a surprise. But we are fully human. Prideful. Insecure. Vengeful at times. Scared. Lonely.

And yes. We answered a call to serve children of God. To tell those children beautiful and true things. You are loved. Worthy. Invited. Fully Alive. Beloved. Forgiven.

Pastors are invited to practice that identity, just like you are. Hopefully, pastors are intentional about that practice and it shows. But many of us (like all humans) figured out early on that it's eerily easy to pull it together on the surface and therefore hide the mess underneath.

I've long been fascinated by clergy cultures and the way we relate to each other. I'm sure it comes from watching my dad's ministry over the years. I was curious about how teams worked together and how people dealt with the chaos of relationships and being the church together. I learned as many of the rules of leadership in the church as I could. I wanted to do it the "right way." Ah, told you I'm an Enneagram One.

The rules about leadership had some uncomfortable ones mixed in. I picked up that leadership included cynicism, isolation, comparison, and competition. I hated that it was true but it felt universal. The discomfort hung in the air we breathed as I navigated seminary and my first few pastoral appointments.

It's human to struggle with comparison, competition, isolation, and cynicism. Our ego shouts all day long for our worth and value, which assumes it comes when someone else looks worse than us. Left unchecked, our ego calls the shots. As I moved through therapy and named many old painful beliefs in my being, these beliefs were the next to fall.

What if we could intentionally practice a different kind of leadership culture? What might it look like to be the opposite of the toxic assumptions we've held for so long about "the way it's always been?"

The Palms Up Leadership Cohort was born. I sat at our dining room table on a June afternoon as it danced across a blank sheet of paper. A nine-month intentionally curated space where leaders can flourish. We deeply value intention, collaboration, curiosity, and joy as we grow together.

As our denomination continues to break open into a new thing, there is a need for peer-led, grassroots, collaborative spaces for leaders to grow together that don't require extensive resource support. We're intentional about making space for established local church pastors and church planters to build relationships. Our first cohort has four local church pastors and three planters.

We are tired of competing with each other. We want to partner together in new ways to grow as humans, followers of Jesus, and leaders in the church. We believe this happens best in relationship with our peers. We believe the collaboration of planters and existing pastors can stretch each other in effective ways for God's community.

This cohort is a safe space to practice the values we hold. It is okay to share something you're proud of without fearing others will feel threatened. It is okay to share the place you're falling apart without fear others will leave you on the ground. We talk practical elements like church budgets, sustainable rhythms, leading a team, preaching themes, community partnerships, and navigating conflict. We laugh a lot.

There's a high expectation around emotional health since it is key to our work with others. Cohort participants are expected to access their mental health benefit for three counseling sessions during the year, to meet with a spiritual director, and practice a Sabbath rhythm.

The first cohort signed up intending to start their own cohort after our first year together. We dream of seven leaders who practice a new culture together and then each begin a cohort to incarnate what they loved about the first one.

As with any dream, it's fun to think about! But who knows how it goes when it's up and running. We certainly didn't anticipate a pandemic being part of our task during this cohort! But I continue to learn so much from this group. They are human beings with pain, fear, gifts, and joy. Spending nine months practicing these new relationships and a new culture was more of a gift than I could imagine.

To Jeremy, Joe, Katy, Alissa, Erin & Kate: Thank you. Thank you for saying yes to an experiment. Thank you for telling your truth and trusting us to catch you. Thank you for teaching me what collaboration can look like across lines we've been told not to cross. Thank you for your texts, encouragement, and your trust.

I'll never forget our very first video call. I sat in my office at church, terrified and nervous. Who are you to think these people want to do this with you?

I took a deep breath, logged in, smiled, and off we went.

Turns out we all needed this more than we knew.

Palms up!

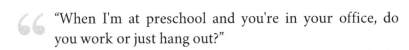

"When I'm at preschool and you're in your office, do you work or just hang out?"

— Isabella

Begin Again

You know the moment where you're
five steps into a new project
and you realize you're stuck?
But you've already told everyone
about this detail
or that
It feels like they're counting on it
Expecting it
You're stuck

And yet

Are they really?

They might have simply nodded along
with your excitement
out of friendship
courtesy

kindness
obligation

Which means you're not actually stuck

You can begin again
No one else gets to decide that
for you

All those plans you prepared
created
dreamed up
were just the first draft
to get you to the next right thing

You have permission
to begin again

13

LOOKING BACK

Sermon Series Highlights | 2015-2020

S omeone once compared preaching to weekly nourishment over a
long period of time. We may not remember the exact phrase or
story that helped our soul rest that day, but we're still deeply grateful
for the moment we took a step toward God. It's hard to believe that
we have traveled through forty-five sermon series together in the past
five years!

Stepping into a pulpit to deliver a sermon is one of the great honors
of serving as pastor. Your time is valuable and pastors don't take it for
granted that you offer it to your church family in this way. Preachers
pray, reflect, look at our own lives, the headlines, consider what we
know about what you're experiencing and out comes a message that
hopefully makes room for us to connect with God in a new way.

As I look back over the series we experienced together, some high-
lights rose to the surface.

Questions Jesus Asked (Fall 2015): The four gospels record 173 questions asked by Jesus. He didn't ask them for his own sake, but for

people who were too afraid or unaware to ask themselves. Jesus' questions in the 1st century can still change our lives today. "Do you love me? Who was a neighbor? Do you want to be healed?"

Hard Questions (Summer 2016): I'll never forget the summer we took eleven weeks and wrestled with some of the most difficult questions of our day: Is it okay to have doubts and questions? What do we do about global warming? Does God care how I vote? How do I understand the Bible if I don't take it all literally? If God loves me just as I am, why would I change? Is Jesus really the only way to God? What happens when I die? Why do bad things happen to good people? What a summer!

I'm So Busy (Fall 2016): We're addicted to being busy. And it's slowly destroying our quality of life with God, others and ourselves. A rich biblical tradition and rhythm holds the key to understanding time differently. This is the one where we unpacked why a Sabbath practice is central to living as a Jesus follower.

Tell Me a Story (February 2017): Many of us have gotten messages from the Bible that have been painful, exclusive and negative. So we chose not to get too involved with it. But what if there are other ways to engage these stories that challenge us in the midst of grace? We're on a mission to embrace the nuance, variety and love found in these stories. May we have the eyes and ears of a child, amazed at the stories of our Creator's love for us.

Journey Into Forgiveness (Lent 2017): Desmond Tutu reminds us, "Forgiveness is nothing less than the way we heal the world. We heal the world by healing each and every one of our hearts. The process is simple, but it is not easy." We set aside six weeks to journey deep into the heart of forgiveness. This was easily the most transformative series for hundreds of us that year.

Waking Up: Moving from Fear to Joy (Easter 2017): This was the message where I finally named the reality of my anxiety and panic. After a long time of internal work, it felt like a miracle to name my story out loud with you. It may have been another sermon to some, but I now label my life as pre-Easter 2017 and post-Easter 2017. It was a transformative day in my personal life. Thank you for allowing me space to share how God was at work in my life.

Summer of Stories (Summer 2017): I loved this series because you all got to share so many of your own stories of faith and trusting God. Our church family still talks about stories we heard that summer.

Live Like You're Loved (Fall 2017): We all feel lost at times. Without direction. We wonder if we should do more good things to earn more points with God or life. We enjoyed exploring a fascinating announcement from Jesus: "You're already at the party." What happens when we live like we're already loved?

Better Together (Lent 2018): Our world feels more divided than ever. We're convinced others are against us. What if we really are better together? What if what we fear in the other is a wakeup call to make space for important conversations? During this Lenten season, we explored what it meant to be a good neighbor when it came to race, gender, politics, generational differences and loving the people of Marysville, Washington.

The Wesley Challenge (Winter 2019): This was the one with all the John Wesley questions! Is Jesus real to me? Am I enjoying prayer? Did the Bible live in me today? We walked through twenty-one of these questions and practiced answering them together with each other. I loved how practical these questions were!

The Gift & Grief of Growth (Spring 2019): Growth of all kinds is a part of life. Sometimes it's welcome. Other times, it's difficult and awkward. For three weeks, we explored the life of Peter, a disciple of Jesus, as he wrestles with invitations to growth and change. We reflected on the gift and grief of growth in our local faith community. It's a good thing when a church grows, but it can also be difficult. The church continued to work through some important conversations as we continued to show up and pay attention to God's invitations together.

Bold Belief (Fall 2019): We went deep into the story of friends carrying a friend to Jesus through the roof. What did it mean to be in proximity to a healing? How do we borrow bold belief from each other? What does it mean to participate in a miracle?

Generations (Fall 2019): It's no secret I love generational intelligence. Every time we talk about it, light bulbs go off and mindsets shift. We walked through the characteristics, communication styles, how each generation connects to God and a vision for intergenerational partnership. Understanding each other gives God more room to work.

Thank you for allowing me the space to serve you in this way for five years. It was the first time I started weekly preaching and by the grace of God I still love it!

Thank you for your grace on the Sundays it was lackluster.

Thank you for sharing your stories so generously with this community.

Thank you for your grace when we didn't see something the same way.

Thank you for your grace when you allowed me to share honestly from my own life the struggle and joy of following Jesus.

Thank you for laughing at stories about my growing children.

Thank you for your emails, texts and letters following a sermon that meant a lot to you. You'll never understand how much this means to preachers.

Thank you for sharing sermons with your loved ones.

Thank you for receiving these stories and ideas into your lives.

It was an absolute honor and joy to partner with you in this way.

Isabella showed me her drawing from Sunday School with colored feet. "God didn't have feet so I gave him feet. And put a band aid on them so he would feel better."

Making Room for Goodbyes | June 23, 2019

My phone was on record while tears traveled down my warm cheeks. My sister sat next to me as sniffles filled our corner of the room. Our brothers and husbands sat behind us next to our mom. In front of us, we watched our dad do something he does well: transitions.

After five years at Bend Church and forty years of full-time ministry, my dad was retiring. He told his church last fall and the new pastor was announced a few months ago. Lots of people worked behind the scenes to plan parties, prepare for their new pastor and celebrate their outgoing pastor. Typically, in the United Methodist Church, the outgoing pastor has a last Sunday and the new pastor arrives a week or two later. They've maybe spoken by phone or email a couple times. Maybe they know each other or they may not.

But it's rare that the outgoing and incoming pastor lead worship together. In the same room. With their beloved community.

There we were, watching our dad invite Bend's new pastor, Jen, up to receive a gift from the church. They prayed together. Dad released everyone to her care and love. Tears flowed. There was forgiveness, closure and a letting go. As Pastor Jen opened her palms, she received the new space to lead and love in this place.

The actual transfer struck such a deep chord in my being. Why?

It wasn't just that I was celebrating Dad's entire active ministry as a United Methodist elder. It went deeper than that.

It was the ritual of saying goodbye.

Our culture doesn't do this well. Life changes all the time and we don't know how to grieve change. We reserve grief for a loved one's death. Not for the loss of a dream, the end of a school year, a changing friendship or the end of a fantastic vacation. Maybe the grief feels too dramatic or we'd rather avoid painful feelings. We move on. We push sadness away or we get stuck in it because we don't know what to do with it.

A few years ago, I intentionally started normalizing goodbyes with our children. I wanted a small ritual so they could let something go and move to the next thing. Whenever we leave for a long trip, we say goodbye to our daughter's room, to the playroom and the entire house. It gives her space to name the goodbye so she can then let it go. There's still sadness and some tears. But she can bring it outside of herself a bit. We can share the goodbye. The naming of the goodbye permits us to feel whatever feelings are inside.

You have permission to say goodbye to the big and small transitions in your life. How might you mark the end of a school year in a meaningful way for a child who's a little sad about leaving friends and excited for the next school year? You can create intentional goodbye moments with neighbors who are moving, the loss of a physical ability or a change in employment.

Saying goodbye doesn't mean the sadness vanishes. If anything, it intensifies for a season. We actually *feel* it. It's the moment many people avoid. But for those willing to step more fully into their grief, they'll find Love, meaning, freedom and new life on the other side.

When I left St. John United Methodist Church in Anchorage, Alaska after sixteen years as part of their church family, I was intentional about saying goodbye. I knew the depth of my goodbye to them would enable me to be ready to say hello to you, my new church family in Marysville, Washington. I preached the sermons, had the conversations, and said all the things I wanted to say. I put into words what they meant to me as a young person who heard a call to ministry and grew to become one of their pastors for a season. I received their kind words and love. I'll never forget my last Sunday with the people of St John's. I stood at the back of the sanctuary and cried and hugged every person. They had carried me through a significant season in my life and I wanted to say goodbye well.

Intentional goodbyes gift us the room for a new hello.

Back to that Sunday in the Bend Church. Dad said his final blessing and then added, "And it's okay to say hi to Pastor Jen." I felt the sense of relief in the room. In that moment, he let go and gave everyone permission to deepen a relationship with their new pastor. People formed lines with both pastors to offer hugs and tears. Laughter filled the room.

It's a beautiful thing to say goodbye. To let go. To open our palms wide to what Love wants to do through us. May we not miss the new invitations because we haven't said goodbye to the old ones.

The Most Important Things to Us | 2018-2020

One of my favorite things I learned in Multiplying Ministries was the power of defining the values of a faith community. What are the most important things to us? When a group of people can get clear about these things, it shapes everything that flows out of them. Our staff team drafted this list, our Vision Team improved it and we reviewed it with people in the church family. Then we talked about it, preached it, created art about it and shared stories about it.

I've been a part of organizations that have done this work but then the list got lost on someone's desk. The power of defining values never made it out of the office.

But with Marysville, something different happened. These came to life. They became part of us. Defining the most important things to us gave us strong boundaries and a field we wanted to play on. Because we knew these, we knew when to say no. We knew when to say yes.

Grace and Love are for all people
God loves all people and families. So do we.

God welcomes our questions and doubts
We grow by staying in hard conversations with God and each other.
We don't back down from our doubts and tough questions. We
journey into them together.

Becoming whole in Christ
We're always in process, learning, challenging, seeking. Our growth as
a disciple of Jesus Christ never ends.

Cultivating a sustainable rhythm
Our world moves fast and God invites us to slow down. We honor the
Sabbath and seek a pace that makes room for the Spirit to move.

Every story matters
Our personal and communal stories matter. We share good news with
Marysville with transparency, honesty and purpose.

Our faith impacts our community
We are the hands and feet of Christ in Marysville and around the
world. Our work for social justice means this love is for all people.

Everyone is in ministry
Each of us have a gift to share and we find our sweet spot to serve and
lead. We disciple leaders who disciple leaders who disciple leaders.

Our purpose matters more than our preference
We give up things we love for people we love even more. It's a joy to
let go of the way it's always been so we can see the new thing God is
doing.

Side note: eight values is a lot. Doing extra work to whittle it down to
four or five would bear even more fruit.

243

During our five years together as a church family, these eight values defined much of our work. It's also helpful to know values can shift over time, especially with new leadership. Many of these qualities were present in the church long before I arrived. But some of them were central to my own values. It's always a dance between pastor and church family as the values get shaped.

It's okay for them to change. God is a living and breathing entity at work in and through us. The people of Marysville United Methodist Church will change. We're continually invited to define the most important things to us if we want to be communities that are clear on our mission in the world.

Join the Journey | 2015-2020

One of my favorite things we did in Marysville was called Join the Journey. Every few months, we invited anyone new to the church over to our home. One, it gave us a reason to clean the house. Two, we attempted to show people who we were as they decided if this was a church family they could trust.

The first few minutes were typically filled with dessert, name tags, children playing in the other room and awkward conversations between people meeting for the first time. We gave house tours, told stories about the home remodels over the years and made sure they knew this was the church's home. We shared our gratitude for getting to live here. We hoped to instill a sense of pride and stewardship in them for the home. It's a beautiful gift to invite their pastoral family to live here!

Once everyone arrives, we each find our seats. Our groups range in size from five to fifteen. One night, we had twenty-four guests so we met at church. After a round of introductions, Aaron and I share part of our story. The details vary but we tell of growing up in pastor's families in Ohio, Florida and Alaska. We tell our story of meeting in Florida at college, getting married, moving to Ohio for seminary and on to Alaska for my first appointment. We tell stories about our kids and the things that make us come alive. We name the things we love about ministry and the things that challenge us. We share what we love about this specific church family. We hope our new friends sense our hearts during this evening. That we can cut through all the assumptions and expectations about what a pastor's family might be like. It's an evening where we invite people to begin to trust us. It's holy ground.

After our sharing, I invite our new friends to share some of their back story, especially their faith journey. The walls in that living room have heard every journey imaginable over five years! Not a single person took a direct route to faith in God and participation in a church community. Many painful stories have spilled out over the years. Stories of loss, heartbreak, doubt, exclusion, disinterest and fear.

You can almost see the bonds forming in real time during this hour and a half together in this living room. Strangers become acquaintances with a door nudged open toward potential friendship. I lean slightly forward in my chair, focusing on every single story and listening to their heart underneath it all. I imagine what it must have felt like to walk that specific journey. My heart overflows with gratitude that we're able to hold safe space where children of God can practice trust in a spiritual leader again. Or for the first time.

I honor the weight of what we hold with people in those moments. The harm churches have done over our years is real. The church is full of imperfect people. Including us! So this practice of trusting each other, even when we know it could fall apart, is a holy moment of trusting love. Even though this will be an imperfect community, are we willing to show up to and for each other? Knowing we will get hurt along the way, do we still want to spend time with this community? Is there space for us to believe differently as we each work out our relationship with God? There are a lot of unspoken questions being asked in these evenings.

There's often a moment in someone's sharing where they affirm their gratitude for this church family and heads around the room nod in agreement. You can see the love and spirit of Jesus present among these new friends. We arrive as separate individuals and leave as people connected by something bigger than our single story. We are becoming a body of Christ.

We near the end of our evening because hard stops are a real thing when young kids are starting to whine! I gather everyone's attention and thank them for sharing part of their evening with us. I offer potential next steps for deeper connection in the church if they're interested. Then I lean in a little bit and say, "Before we pray together, I want to tell you that I would love to be your pastor. I know what a big deal it is to trust someone with your relationship with God. I'll do my best to honor the sacredness of this call. And I happen to know a church family who would be delighted to welcome you in. Our church family would be stronger with you a part of it. Know also that we value releasing the outcome. So you're also welcome to engage in whatever way feels best for you in each season."

"Can I pray for you?" Heads nod and eyes close.

"God, thank you for each person gathered in this room tonight.

Thank you for the kids who remind us to play and laugh. Thank you for the food that deepens our connection to you and each other. Thank you for the journeys shared tonight. Thank you for the twists and turns that bring us to this moment. We would be honored to walk with each other for a season as we seek to become deeply faithful followers of you and your son, Jesus Christ. We hold the gifts of this church family loosely with great joy and trust. God, we are yours. And all God's children said? Amen."

To the one hundred and fifty-three of you who experienced a Join the Journey evening with our family, thank you. Your stories taught me so much about how we become a church family together. Your trust in me felt like gift, never burden. Your love of God gave me life. Your curiosity about faith spurred me on in deeper quest. This was never just a "get to know the pastor" kind of thing. This was risking trust together. And I'm forever grateful for these moments we shared.

Here's to the journey.

Marysville Globe | 2017-2020

Toward the end of our Better Together sermon series during Lent 2017, Steve Powell, our Song Team drummer, asked if I'd be interested in adapting the content of that series into articles for our local paper, The Marysville Globe. Steve happened to be the editor of the paper and was looking for a spiritual voice to offer commentary to our town. I jumped at the opportunity to share what we were learning, but was unsure that jumping into race, gender and politics was a great way to make friends. We went for it anyways and it became the beginning of almost thirty articles written for the Globe over three years.

It was a unique writing experience because there weren't comments available at the bottom of the articles so I rarely got feedback (or pushback). It was the ultimate release the outcome exercise. I enjoyed adapting blog articles, sermon themes and devotional pieces into language our Marysville friends might resonate with.

I knew there were plenty of Jesus followers in town who don't interpret the Bible in the way we do but I continued to let that go each time I hit "Send." They weren't my audience anyways. I wrote for the people who felt spiritual but wanted nothing to do with the church. I was hopeful that some of our stories over these three years softened the ground for friends. Maybe church was worth the exploration again. And not that we've got everything figured out. We have our issues and conflict since, well, we're human. I wrote for the people who knew there had to be more to the Jesus story than judgment and condemnation. I wrote for the people looking for spiritual practices on a Tuesday morning or Friday night.

Thank you to Steve for trusting me with space in our paper. Here's to all the creative ways we tell stories of grace and love!

 "Wesley, why do you talk to me so much?"

— ISABELLA

The Real Rock Stars | May 12, 2019

Today, I need to name and celebrate the twelve faith communities who taught me all kinds of beautiful ways to love people and practice the way of Jesus:

- Hume UMC in Lima, Ohio
- Trinity UMC in Lima, Ohio
- Soldotna UMC in Soldotna, Alaska

- St. John UMC in Anchorage, Alaska
- Florida Southern College in Lakeland, Florida
- Georgianna UMC in Merritt Island, Florida
- First UMC Cocoa, Cocoa, Florida
- United Theological Seminary in Dayton, Ohio
- Stillwater Church in Dayton, Ohio
- East Anchorage UMC, Anchorage, Alaska
- Anchor Park UMC, Anchorage, Alaska
- Marysville UMC, Marysville, Washington

The United Methodist movement has shaped me deeply. I said yes to a call to ordained ministry when I was 17 years old at Exploration, a national gathering for United Methodist students considering a call to ministry. Twelve years later, I was ordained an elder in the United Methodist Church.

When I graduated from United Theological Seminary and became a pastor, I never would have thought I'd serve a reconciling congregation. We were part of a global church that didn't agree on human sexuality. I thought the pastors who led those churches were incredibly brave and strong.

And then I got to know Ryan, Debbie, Lisa, Susan, Barb, Sabrina, Heather, Monica, Donnie, Anthony, Kevin, Lynn, Gail, Wendy, Mandi, Marisa, Stephanie, Joy, Brian, Michael, Teri, Richard, Karen & many other friends who at some point decided that to be whole in the eyes of the One who made them, they could no longer ignore their true selves. Then I realized, it's not the pastor of the reconciling church that's super brave. It's the members of a reconciling church who are freaking rock stars.

They continue to say yes to God even while so many people tell them no.

They walk in the doors terrified and uncomfortable, but they still show up.

Love draws them out of their fear and into communities who know how incredible they are.

Couples stand in the back and nervously hold hands in worship waiting to see if someone will give them an awkward stare. And when none come, they sink more deeply into their skin and feel at home.

It's beautiful to watch straight friends who sometimes get it and those who still aren't quite there, throw out the red carpet, invite friends to groups and over for dinner.

And pastors of reconciling churches never tire of hearing the same comment from just about every new member: "I didn't know a place like this existed."

Yes, dear friends, they exist. And may I let you in on a little secret? They don't simply exist. They are thriving, bursting with life, and overflowing with the movement of God. This church family in the Pacific Northwest experiences baptisms, new members, 30% increase in worship attendance, adding a third service, and pledging gifts increasing by 49% in four years.

During the 2019 United Methodist General Conference gathering, they voted to prioritize pension benefits and a traditional under-standing of human sexuality above plans for inclusion. The same day, a guy in our town who has been watching worship online for a month messaged me and asked if he could find out more about baptism. He said, "I grew up going to church when I was younger, but as I strug-gled a lot with my sexuality it kind of scared me away from God and the church. I have found that with the acceptance of your church I am feeling comfortable rediscovering those roots."

It's one reason why it's so painful to watch so many disregard us. I cannot reconcile the absolute fruit and growth of the faith community I serve while others believe it is evil and sinful.

The least I can do is keep telling the story of what I'm seeing in this local church. Because God is up to something incredible in the world and I'm delighted to have a front row seat to it, even if that means our denominational labels change or fall away.

May we all continue to have a front row seat to the movement of God, wherever life takes us. Today, I am thankful for each church who shaped me. They all believed different things about human sexuality and that's okay. Grace and love. It's a journey. But please do not close the Church to communities like mine simply because we have a different interpretation of our holy stories.

We recently received a gift of artwork to hang in the church lobby. It's a beautiful rainbow-colored heart. It was given to our church by a friend my age who was raised to understand human sexuality differently. When the church decided to become reconciling, he stayed away for a while. But then he got to know Mandi and Marisa, an energetic and hilarious couple, his heart shifted. He saw this beautiful piece of artwork in a local store, bought it and asked me to hang it in our church lobby. Every day I see this piece of art and I'm reminded of the apostle Paul who tells us that when we're in step with God, labels fall to the ground. And it happens even when we're in relationship with someone we don't understand.

Here's to the power of what love can do.

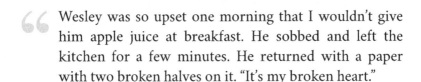

Wesley was so upset one morning that I wouldn't give him apple juice at breakfast. He sobbed and left the kitchen for a few minutes. He returned with a paper with two broken halves on it. "It's my broken heart."

14

THANK YOU AND GOODBYE

***A Prayer for Churches Saying Goodbye During a
Pandemic***

How do you say goodbye
In a time when you
Can't be together?

No hugs
No together tears
No laughter
No meals
In embodied community
Which is the core of who we are?

We do what humans do
Adapt
Innovate
Lean in
Make it up as we go

We get honest about the difficulty of this
And how much we'd prefer to ignore it

Instead, what if we learned something new
About saying goodbye
In a time we can't be together?

Might we stumble into new ways
Of showing our love for each other?
Our gratitude for time spent in community?
For the ways we've challenged and comforted each other?

We don't know what those ways are yet
But we know God will inspire us
Because we practice
Showing up
Paying attention
Cooperating with God
And releasing the outcome
Palms up

Yes, this goodbye is unlike the others
And yet, it can still be a good bye
It's tempting to skip this invitation
Because there's so much
Too much
To hold lately

But what if a blessing waits inside this
Awkward task?

Waiting for us to uncover
A new way to say goodbye?

To say, "Thank you."

To say, "It meant the world."
To say, "We love you."
To say, "We'll miss you."
And to say, "It'll be okay. We're in good hands."

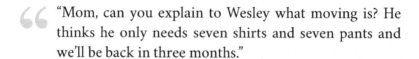 "Mom, can you explain to Wesley what moving is? He thinks he only needs seven shirts and seven pants and we'll be back in three months."

— ISABELLA

My Forest is Becoming a Neighborhood

I love walking through the neighborhoods around the parsonage, our home for these past five years. On these walks, sermons have poured forth, tears fell, phone calls were enjoyed and I nodded to my fellow humans.

A month or two after we moved here, I found a large area of trees and forest in the next neighborhood over. It called my name like cookies in the freezer do. I wanted to explore this small forest but there was a large No Trespassing sign posted by a very well-worn path into the woods. So I did what any Enneagram One would do. I took three steps past the sign, just inside the forest, and took a deep breath. I was home. I never went farther than those three steps in because I couldn't stand the idea of getting in trouble, yet I needed these trees.

I visited the trees in the rain and listened to the drops hit the leaves. I visited the trees in the early morning fog as the sun rose through the cracks in the forest. I visited the trees in the late summer evening and watched the sun go to sleep after a long warm day. I visited the trees when I was sad. When I was happy. When I was stuck. I visited the trees with my earbuds in and did a few yoga poses as I enjoyed this peaceful home. I knew this was one place I could go where I could breathe deeply again.

It turns out those trees had a name. Spook Woods. A woman from out of state owned the property. There are lots of stories of teenagers over the years getting into trouble in those protected woods. Then a teenager died in those woods in an after school fight. A week after that, I stood on the edge of the woods, three steps in, and cried. This place where I could breathe had been used to kill. I lifted the family in prayer, the kids who experienced that moment, and all in our community who see violence as a solution to anything. The trees didn't respond when I cried out in anger. But I imagine they weep along with us.

A little later, we saw a new sign go up on the edge of the property. Someone wanted to develop it for housing. There was a number to call with questions or concerns. I thought often about calling to register my concern. The trees were beautiful and healing. I couldn't bear the thought of them all coming down. But I also knew the difficult stories coming from those woods and that keeping them didn't feel wise either.

One day, we drove by and saw a fence up. A new sign was posted. It was officially becoming a space for thirty new homes. As the kids and I got back in the car, I told them I felt sad. Our four-year-old buckled his seatbelt and said, "I don't want anyone to take down the trees." A few tears rolled down my cheeks as I backed up the van and we drove off.

I returned the next morning by myself to take my three steps in, just past the sign. I breathed deeply. I cried. I thanked God for this gift of space for the past four years.

At first, those trees felt like my trees. But then I stood there and imagined a home and a paved street and kids playing. I imagined a new community. I wondered if I'd become friends with new residents. And my heart softened. Maybe I could grieve this loss and come to see a bigger purpose for this land.

Over the next months, I continued to walk to the edge of the fence and watch. Tree by tree, they hit the ground. I cried. I took pictures of the spot I loved because I knew it would quickly become pavement. As more trees fell, were cleared away and gravel brought in, we continued to watch. And slowly but surely, my heart was shifting. I went from holding my sacred space tightly and possessively to making some room for it to become new.

The city didn't need my permission. The landowner didn't either. But for my participation in my neighborhood, I needed to permit my heart to let this sacred space go. It was never about God living in those trees. It was simply a place where I had meaningful connections with our Creator and I came to locate God in that space. But God is also present over in the trees of Jennings Park. And the water by the Ebey Waterfront trail. And the marina water in Everett. And the water at Kayak Point. I chose to open my heart in gratitude instead of staying stuck on my preferences for my little illegal prayer spot.

Then each day, as more and more trees hit the ground and were dragged into piles, the entire horizon of our neighborhood changed. You don't realize how often you look at something until it's not there. There was a void in the skyline. It felt weird. Part of me wanted to avoid that street. But a bigger part of me was fascinated as to why I cared so much. Each day I would walk or drive to the edge and look. I watched the forest diminish. I kept a close eye on it as it changed. And each day, it got easier. I was getting used to the new thing. I kept my eyes on it. I refused to look away. Different angles. Perspectives.

Turns out I was saying goodbye each time I adjusted to what was ending. I learned a lot about change, loss, and transition in those long months of construction. It was okay to let go of something I loved. It didn't change the truth that it happened and meant a lot to me.

To my trees that are long gone: Thank you for being there when I needed it. I'm going to miss you. You sustained me in countless moments. You helped me breathe when I was afraid. You gently loved me without demand. Your presence helped me become more of myself. Thank you for witnessing the tears, the joy, the growth, and the fear. Like God, your presence healed me.

As we slowly pack up our home to move to Edmonds, guess how this sacred space continues to love me? Seven of the homes are complete. The road is paved and includes lots of sidewalks. During quarantine, we take the kids there to ride bikes most evenings. They zoom around and laugh in this wide-open space. This land continues to love and serve my family, even as it changes.

I take walks through the neighborhood. The openness and expansiveness of that plot of land inspires me now. My music swells, I look up and feel alive as the sky surrounds.

I come to the spot on the pavement where the sign used to be. I take three steps in and pause. God, thank you for this spot where I encountered you so faithfully. I release it to you. As it becomes new, may you continue to love your people in wildly creative ways.

And I look forward to finding new spots in Edmonds where God will meet me in just the way I'll need in that season. Here's to the sacred spaces that serve us all. May we hold them loosely with gratitude and joy.

If Walls Could Speak

Thank you, God, for each person who nervously stood in the sanctuary to share their story. Their courage helped us see you more clearly.

Thank you, God, for each note played and sung in this holy space. Each musician is a mouthpiece for your love.

Thank you, God, for the kind souls who've turned on microphones, poured grape juice, set up the baptismal font, refilled candles, rearranged chairs, passed out bulletins, introduced themselves and said hi to a new friend. They are the hands and feet of Jesus.

Thank you, God, for the countless moments I stood before a community looking for a moment of hope. Little did they know they were giving me hope.

Thank you, God, for each gathering in the Green Room these past five years. Workshops on marriage, anxiety, meditation, depression, yoga, social justice, leadership, and dreaming of a new future filled this space. Thank you for new questions, conversations while our kids played and enough food to feed an army. Thank you for the laughter during variety shows and chili cook-offs. Thank you for how this room meets so many of our needs for embodied community.

Thank you, God for our choir room that hosts space for endless conversations of faith. Thank you for the new friends made in this space, the curious questions that emerged, and the joy of community groups connecting.

Thank you, God, for our youth room. For the safety and trust felt in this room, we give you thanks. For a space where teens can question, wonder, vent, and laugh, we are thankful. Bless each teen who moves through this space. May they feel safe and held in the arms of God.

Thank you, God, for the sound of laughter on our playground. We're thankful for bodies that move and play. Thank you for the hours of swinging, sliding, and creating hosted in this space. May children feel delight and love in this beautiful outdoor space.

Thank you, God, for the pure joy that rings out from our nursery. It's been a place of safety and play for so many families. Thank you for how this space cared for our children in the early days. Thank you for the playgroups, the late nights, the art projects, and the love that fills this space.

Thank you, God, for the library and the grieving families who've gathered here. Thank you for the groups who've grown here and the leadership conversations that invited us forward. For the preschool staff lunches, staff meetings, and community groups who found this space inviting, we give you thanks.

Thank you, God, for the preschool classrooms and Sunday School spaces that house little ones. For twenty years, we've welcomed families through these doors and into safety and growth. For paintings, learning to cut with scissors and music, we give thanks.

Thank you, God, for our kitchen that feeds us so well. For the groups who bond over food and their week, we give thanks. Continue to heal and feed your beloved children through this space.

Thank you, God, for our narthex that welcomes weary souls to rest and connect. We give you thanks for every conversation that spills out in this holy space.

Thank you, God, for our office where passionate hearts work together to support this community. For the heavy hearts that enter and leave lighter, we give you thanks. Laughter, teamwork, and deep love for church family fills this space.

Thank you, God, for our Kloz 4 Kids space. We give thanks for families who pick out new clothing for their children. Grant each family courage, confidence, and love as they leave this space.

Thank you, God for our Miracle House. We're delighted to welcome each family as they take another step toward becoming whole. May their rest be deep, worries light, and joy overflowing.

God, your church is not a building, it's a people. And we are deeply grateful for the building that enables so much of your church to exist. If these walls could speak, they'd tell story after story of your grace and your love.

My Wise Guys

Every pastor needs a team of wise guys. You know, the ones who are extra smart about things the pastor may not know. The ones who know the church inside and out. The ones who give extra time to listening, untangling an issue, and moving us forward with grace.

I sometimes wonder what it's like for men in their 50s-70s to have a female pastor in her 30s. If I'm them, I might think of myself as a daughter more than a pastor. I'd struggle to take me seriously. I've had less time to experience life, make mistakes, learn from them, and lead others. I'm not great at shooting the breeze because once we venture beyond Seahawk football stats, I'm not the best conversation partner. So I've always been mindful of the potential relationship gap between us. Could they connect with God through my preaching? What illustrations might I share that connects to their life experience? What characteristics of God might they hear anew because it's through a 37-year-old woman?

But my wise guys? It felt like I had their utmost respect and love. They sent encouraging emails and texts after sermons that may have ruffled some feathers in the best way. They stopped by the office just to say hi. They called to run a question or issue by me and then stayed on the phone for a minute to see how my kids were doing. They never tore me down when I dropped the ball on something. They spoke up for me when I wasn't present in a conversation. They gave me high fives in the hallways.

A few of my wise guys are retired clergy and they could have written the book on how to do this well. It's quite a dance for a retired clergy person to honor the call that still lights a fire in them with the reality that another leader has the lead in this community. I can only hope and pray that when I retire, I remember to honor my new pastor the way they've supported me. They knew the really hard parts of this job and could affirm me in those seasons. They knew the joy of baptisms, communion, weddings, and preaching. I won the lottery when it comes to retired clergy.

And best of all, they were all my coaching team. They taught and strengthened so many of my skill sets. The ones they never teach you in seminary. Because of them, I've got a fighting chance at navigating budget documents, payroll, insurance, stewardship season, capital projects, endowments, and scheduling long-term maintenance on the building.

These guys would have been well within their rights to roll their eyes at me on multiple occasions. But they never did, that I saw. They never spoke down to me in a condescending way. These guys taught me what they knew, asked questions when they didn't know something, and cheered me every single step of the way.

I'm going to miss these guys. I loved them. I loved our teamwork and the ways they made this faith community stronger. Here's to the wise guys among us all!

My Wise Women

I would be curled up in a ball in the corner of my bedroom closet if it weren't for my wise women. These women have held me up in every moment I felt lost, frustrated, or overwhelmed. They've called, listened, taken me out to breakfast, affirmed the tears, and whispered me back to life. These women have always seen something in me that I didn't yet see.

They were interesting relationships because I thought they needed me to be some wise sage superwoman pastor who had her life together. These women never once let me believe that was a thing. They called me on it every single time. They gently prodded when they sensed I wasn't doing great. After a while, I stopped trying to get it past them. I gave up. Surrendered.

Then I could finally accept this gift for what it was. God gifted wise women to sustain, strengthen and encourage me. Some days I wondered if I wasn't here for them. Maybe they were just here for me. But then, in the weirdness of God's economy, they connected with God through me too. Love really can use anyone and everything to convey grace and joy. Even when people are wildly unaware they're being a home for God.

I don't know how I'll ever convey how much these wise women meant to me during these past five years. Like Aaron holding up Moses' arms so God could keep using him, my wise women picked me up off the ground countless times. Their attentive grace enabled complexity to unravel. Their kindness soothed the places that ached. Their accountability reminded me God was always capable of more than our limited minds could imagine. Their counsel hemmed me in when I wandered a bit too far away.

Sometimes I got so busy helping others see that we don't have to compete with each other, that I missed the truth of these wise women. We learned together that the comparison game is a waste of time, isolation isn't the solution, and cynicism is just fear shaking in its boots. We were practicing the very things I so wanted to see in the world. Sometimes I fear I was so busy doing the things that I missed the true power of these wise women. *Did I slow down enough to enjoy the gift while offering the gift to others?* This is forever a question for spiritual leaders.

To my wise women who I can't see right now, thank you.

I'm not sure you'll ever know the depth to which your love gave me life in this season. Your trust and belief in me was ridiculous and I reminded you of this often. But thank you for seeing what I couldn't yet see. Thank you for your texts, emails, phone calls, notes, meals, laughter, tears, and nodding, "me too."

Because of you, I felt held as I served others.

Because of you, I know this faith community will be held as I let go.

Because of you, when I think of Marysville for the rest of my life, I'll smile with deep gratitude.

Because of you, we got to witness the changing of lives.

Because of you, more love exists in the world.

Amen.

Our Team

I frequently told people Tuesdays at 9:30 am was one of my favorite times of the week. Staff meetings! For the last decade or two, I've always loved any time leadership teams gather. I'm fascinated by the dynamics, the encouragement, the support, the coaching, and the potential for honest and transparent growth as a team. And this team at Marysville UMC was my favorite one yet.

A few minutes before 9:30 am, members trickle into the office. When I first arrived, we met in the library but soon shifted to my office after I moved more chairs in. It felt comfortable and cozy. As many people pointed out, it also felt dark. I was going for safe and welcoming, but using lamps instead of the overhead fluorescent lights was a source of constant jokes. Mostly by our worship leader.

Everyone had their spots and rarely switched it up. We joked and laughed and shared about the peculiarities of our daily lives. We know each other's kids and partners. We know the heavy stuff that's hard to talk about. We know what we're looking forward to. This was our small group.

We started our meetings by checking in with each other around a variety of prompts. Some days it was our team verse, Romans 12:11-13 in the Message version. Some days it was highs and lows from our personal or work lives. Some mornings, we opened with silence and prayer.

One of my favorite conversations with our staff was inviting wins connected to values. We took turns naming a win we saw in someone else's ministry area and connected it to one of our values. Over the years, it became second nature to look for the good in each other and to name it. We practiced this week in and week out. What a gift!

We coordinated details for upcoming events, brainstormed on tricky issues, and pitched ideas to each other. We practiced honesty when something wasn't going well. We called ourselves out when we could do better. We prayed for our church family. We wondered where God wanted to take us next and how we might prepare for the journey.

To each person who spent time on our staff team, thank you. It was a holy and sacred time for me. I pray it was meaningful for you as well. I always wrestled with how much to share of myself as a new lead pastor finding her footing, and you cheered me on the whole way. I made mistakes. Plenty of them. You loved me still. I will always look back on these five years with gratitude, joy, and deep love for each of you. Serving with you was the joy of my life.

Tanya

There was someone on our team who taught me more than I realized at the time. I think she might say the same about me. In a way, it's bittersweet that we realized it on the slow side, but it's no less beautiful.

I got a front-row seat to watching Tanya morph from youth pastor to guest preacher to pastoral care lead to licensed local pastor and now to associate pastor. The wonderful thing about Tanya is she's a powerful force but doesn't yet know her strength. Her passion and love for God and all things body of Christ is contagious. Tanya is a wonderful Bible teacher, a brilliant skeptic, and our resident Gen-Xer.

This is all housed inside a heart that deeply knows Spirit, yet sometimes challenges the invitation.

I learned so much from supporting her over the last five years. We are wildly different people. I move fast. Too fast, sometimes. Tanya had questions, wonderings, and commentary. I needed that. I needed someone to slow me down. To double-check an assumption before charging forward. I have several people like this in my life and they can irritate me at times because the questions wet blanket the energy coursing through my being. And yet, I needed Tanya. Her gift mix and skill set were precisely what balanced our team. I was an effective pastor because of her.

Early on, I shared some of my struggles with anxiety with her. At the time, I particularly struggled in hospital settings. Turns out that's where Tanya comes alive. God built her to be a chaplain. To sit with people when they're anxious and hurting. She took the lead on all things pastoral care. It was a joy for me to support her in that work and for Tanya to get the experience coordinating that ministry.

I will never forget doing book studies with Tanya and our team this past year. Without fail, we'd all share our takeaways from a certain chapter and then turn to Tanya and await her critique. After adjusting her reading glasses, she'd launch into a hilarious rebuttal of what we'd read. Complete with comical frustration and disbelief, Tanya had a way of seeing what I didn't see but needed to. Tanya was my extra set of eyes.

We both grew up pastor's kids in the United Methodist Church, which means we have a mutual understanding of how we got to this place in ministry. We know parsonages, frequent moves, being loved by local churches, and seeing the behind-the-scenes conflicts. If my bones are made for innovation, then Tanya's bones are built with a sacred and deep appreciation for our tradition. Tanya knows where we came from.

I needed this perspective on the team even when it altered my plans.

We had many conversations where I was ready to make a drastic change in a ministry or a vision moving forward. I would run it by Tanya, assuming my charisma and excitement would win her over.

It never did.

Tanya saw right through the dramatic joy and possibility to the heart of the question at hand. Was this wise? How did we get to where we are? What needs to be upheld, even if it's not where we want it yet? And she asked these questions with kindness and respect. Which made me slow down and listen. Tanya single-handedly saved me from many leadership mistakes.

Tanya brought things to the front that I would have instinctively ignored. She helped me see the depth and diversity of the kingdom of God in ways I couldn't see from my vantage point. It was uncomfortable at times, but also a gift, to have someone on the team who reminded me of the historic values we held.

From day one, Tanya and I engaged in a silent conversation about hierarchy and collaboration. I instinctively wanted to collaborate on everything. Tanya wanted me to be the boss and tell her what I needed. It took me several years to finally become the more directive supervisor she needed. And I watched Tanya come to see why I loved collaboration so much. People on a team could partner together and leave egos at the door. We could get to a far more beautiful place when everyone's gifts at the table were recognized.

In these past months, Tanya and I feel the loss of not getting to work together in this setting in the future. We know the unknowns of the appointment system but still hoped we had lots of time together. In some ways, it feels like we're starting to truly understand each other. It's bittersweet. And yet, prevenient grace is a thing. Tanya and I were a true team, before we both even realized it. God used us to balance each other. To cheer each other on. To slow me down. To speed her up. To love the people of Marysville United Methodist Church in this season.

Tanya, what a gift you are to me.
Thank you, friend, for walking this road with me.
You shaped me into a more whole version of myself.
Watching God move through you is fascinating.
And I'm forever grateful for our time together.

Kate

February 6, 2016: "Good evening, Pastor Jenny. Kate Kilroy here. I was the guest in the red dress this morning with the large family. I really enjoyed the service today. I will be doing more research on the Methodist denomination as this organization is new to me. That said, I was so taken with the website. So much of what I read I so very personally identified with. And now having met you, I feel assured the website sincerely reflects the heart and mission of the church. So thankful. I am wondering if there is an hour or so you have open where I might meet with you?"

From the day Kate walked in the door, there was something about her spirit that lit up our church family. You may think it's her wild energy, big hugs, funny voices, or an uncanny ability to talk like Ernie. And you'd be right. But it's also her heart. If you've been lucky enough to engage with Kate when she's not bouncing off the walls, then you know what I'm talking about.

This child of God swims in deep waters of faith. Her connection to the Holy Spirit is profound and obvious. I'm not sure I can put into words what she has called forth from my heart with her questions, her bold belief, her Spirit expectations, her genuine support, and her dreams of what's possible.

Kate came from a different faith tradition than me. She'll write a book one day and I hope you'll get to hear the story straight from her. But for now, know that we couldn't be more different when it comes to our childhood experience of faith, of grace, of God. To welcome her first as a guest was a joy. Like all guests through the doors of this church, we love hearing new stories, long-held questions and difficult doubts.

But it quickly became apparent that Kate wasn't your typical guest. God was calling her to something. I didn't know what it was but I knew we could help fan the flame a bit.

Much to my surprise, our Director of Family Ministries soon shared she was receiving a pastoral appointment in Oregon and would be leaving in a few months. We wondered how we'd find a new director. Then I remembered that Kate had served as a children's pastor for hundreds of kids at a mega-church nearby. Hmm. Really, God? Is this a good idea? She's just learning who we are as United Methodists. What it means to step into progressive Christianity. To deconstruct faith and put together a new framework. She wants time to heal and rest.

After lots of honest conversations and discernment, the interview process moved forward and our team offered Kate the position of Director of Family Ministries. She delightfully said yes. We stood in the hallway with some folks after a meeting and I remember saying, "Thank you for all the ways you will share love with the kids of our community. And as a mom, thank you for teaching my kids about Jesus. Thank you for being their pastor." My voice shook for a moment with the power of that sentiment. I trusted Kate with the faith development of my children. What a gift people in children's ministry give to our families.

Over the next year and a half, Kate served this community faithfully. We were not without our challenges though. Our energies are wildly different. I'll never forget a staff conversation we had about moving the choir loft and the Song Team set up in the sanctuary for a season. Each staff person weighed in with their perspective. This was going to be my decision to make. Yet, I was still getting used to Kate's energy. As Tanya recently said, "Kate can sell dirt." This woman can pitch an idea and vision as if it's already true. I sometimes struggle to say what I feel. It would have been easy to step into passive-aggressive mode and dance around it. But, I knew the gift Kate was to this team and community and I had a clear invitation to deepen our partnership and practice honesty. I did and we both learned a lot about each other that day. I learned I can say no to Kate! She learned it's okay to be passionate and hold the outcome loosely.

Kate and I worked hard to name the different hats we wore with each other. She'd walk into the office and immediately say, "I need your pastor hat," or "can you wear your boss hat for a minute?" Because she so clearly knew these boundaries in her own life, she taught me how to navigate the dual roles more effectively.

Then because I sensed her spirit was strong and her trust in God ran deep, she had a front-row seat to how I fell apart in early 2017. In a sense, Kate's arrival at Marysville United Methodist Church started with us holding her as she let the pieces of her life fall to the ground. We cheered her on as she slowly crafted a faith and a journey with Jesus that fit her new life. Then I (quietly) fell apart and she caught me. When I couldn't yet be direct with our church, a few people around me knew how much I was struggling. She covered for me in moments I had to step away because the panic was winning. Kate welcomed my text messages filled with fear and she told me who I was.

And I think that's one of the best gifts Kate gave me. For four years straight, she was my mirror. Not the wild funhouse mirror kind, but the God mirror kind. Kate saw the real me. She was the first to tell me the true story of my heart when I couldn't access it. When I thought the fear would win, she graciously and consistently told me I was a beloved child of God. When I was confused and discouraged, she told a better story of what was unfolding. Kate gave me context and grounding when I was adrift and afraid.

There's power in letting someone see you hit rock bottom. When you muster the strength to look up and see who was willing to sit nearby and offer kindness when you were at your worst? That person is gold.

Especially when my rock bottom wasn't visible from the outside to most people. I was functional. I continued to do my job and love it. I just also happened to be journeying into parts of myself I've kept locked up for decades. And I was terrified. I was questioning everything in the best way and trying to manage panic attacks in the middle of meetings. But she was someone who was part of the road I was walking. I'll never be able to say thank you enough for the support in that season.

As we moved into the fall of 2017, new energy was bubbling around multiplication as a church. As I felt God inviting me to wrestle with some baggage around church growth, I saw new pathways open up. As the 10 in 30 vision emerged, someone at our conference office suggested Kate go through their planter assessment. Kate and I doubted that would go anywhere but thought it couldn't hurt. Turns out, God built Kate to be a church planter too! They identified clear gifting for church planting (which is not easy!). As momentum grew in the church around multiplying, conversations deepened around Kate's potential role. Could she be our first planter? The Bishop and her team said yes. They offered her an appointment.

I'll never forget the day we met at my home. We sat on the couch and I got to tell her the news. And after every single twist and turn in her story, she got to hear that a full time church planter position was available. The tears of gratitude that fell weren't just for that moment. It was like God reached right back into her past and whispered, "Child, you are called. To lead. To love. To serve. No matter what they told you before, this is what is true. It's always been true."

For the past two years, we navigated another change in our relationship. We became colleagues. I was no longer her direct supervisor but now an informal mentor and head cheerleader for seeing what might be possible in our community. Video messages kept us connected through the chaos and joy of church planting. Hours spent discerning, listening, and asking new questions about what faith community could look like if it didn't look like what we thought it had to. This season together had its challenges as we navigated unknown territory at every turn.

And yet, we continued to be mirrors for each other. I would remind her of who she was. I'd whisper God's love for her and this call. I'd give her context and bring her back to the present moment and the invitation in front of us. She did the same for me when I was unclear and uncertain. We still found a way to name the hat we needed at the moment.

"Can you be my pastor for a moment?"

"I need a friend moment. Can I share something?"

"If you were my boss, what would you say about this?"

"As a colleague, can you hold this with me?"

> *Kate, thank you. For all of it.*
> *The gifts you gave me will forever shape who I become.*
> *Watching God work in you is pure joy.*
> *Thank you for loving us so freely.*
> *It mattered.*

To the Ones Who Came Before and the Ones to Come

First, a word to the pastors who've served this community. Thank you. Thank you for the countless Sundays you rose from your chair and stepped to the front of the room and offered what Spirit stirred up in you. Thank you for the hallway conversations, the narthex side hugs, the long meetings spent caring for this community.

Thank you for the difficult conversations you walked into, knowing they were the right ones for that season. Thank you for walking the lonely road of leadership in seasons when people didn't have the full story.

Thank you for the questions you asked that stirred up imagination. Thank you for holding up a mirror so these beloved ones could see how God sees them.

Thank you for throwing seeds around with abandon. You never knew which ones would find healthy soil and take root down deep. Or which ones landed, only to be quickly brushed aside.

Thank you for the risks you took, trusting God's leading in that season. You had no idea what would come next. Still, you took one more step forward and they followed you.

It has been an absolute honor to receive the watering can from you. It's been so much fun to water and nurture the seeds you planted in this community. I got to watch some people bloom and come alive in these five years, due to seeds you planted decades ago.

I'm so thankful to be in this work together.

Second, a word to the pastors to come. Wow. First, I apologize for the lack of filing abilities. I love people and the idea of organization, but the actual organization of the work? The team saved me every single time. So thanks for your grace on pastoral records from 2015-2020.

Thank you for the work you will do in this place and with these people. They're amazing. I'm excited you'll get to water seeds that I helped plant. I'm thankful you'll throw more seeds with wild abandon.

There are things we worked on in these five years that mean the world to me. I want you to know you have all the freedom in the world to let those things go. If you don't sense the energy is there and there are new rustlings of the Spirit, follow those!

Thank you for caring for these people I've come to love. I'll miss them dearly. Knowing you'll stand by their bedside, officiate at their weddings, and welcome their babies gives me unspeakable joy. What a beautiful story that we get to partner together to love this community without serving together at the same time.

Take them on wild adventures! A few of them may grumble, but I think they secretly liked being stretched and challenged to take big risks. Or at least, that's the story I'll tell myself for years to come.

Thank you for teaching them to rest, play, and not save the world all the time. I hope the love of sustainability echoes in their hearts for years to come.

Thank you for taking care of this staff team. They've been a highlight of our time here. They'll cheer you on, offer grace to your flaws, and trust God in you. Feed them well and you're set.

The leaders in this church community are ridiculously wise. They've led this body through challenging seasons and somehow emerged with hope and possibility.

One day, many years from now, I'll wander the halls of this church building. The memories will come rushing back. I'll smile. Laugh. Tears will fall. And I'll remember. All the incredible work that went into these five years and I'll thank God for the seeds planted, watered, and harvested. I'll thank God for the people we all got to love for this season.

We thought we were teaching them about the love of God.

Turns out they were teaching us too.

Take care, future lovers of this community. I release them to you. Love them well. It might just be the adventure of a lifetime.

You Loved Our Kids

How do I say thank you for the most important gift you could have given me as your pastor? You loved our kids. You were patient with them when they felt shy. You gave them treats in the office. You scheduled meetings around school drop off and pick up so I could be fully present to them in those moments. You never seemed to mind their jackets, snacks, and artwork strewn about my office at times. You made room for me to nurse my infant son in between worship services. You gave us a gift that will pay dividends for the rest of their lives.

I got to hire two Family Ministry directors during our time here and I said to both of them through choked tears at the end of our hiring conversation, "Thank you for showing my kids who Jesus is and what love looks like. Their mom is a pastor so it's hard for them to hear it from me sometimes. Thank you for being my kids' pastor."

Thank you for watching them in between services so they wouldn't terrorize people in the hallways. Thank you for serving them communion. Thank you for telling them they're loved. Thank you for teaching their Vacation Bible School classes. Thank you for caring for them in the nursery. Thank you for babysitting them so Aaron and I could go on a date. Thank you for bringing them joy.

And maybe most of all, thank you for keeping my daughter safe. An anaphylactic peanut allergy is no joke and it was tempting to worry she was accidentally eating peanut butter cookies in the Green Room while I was preaching in the sanctuary. But I trusted so many of you who cared for her. Because you took care of her, I could be fully present to our church family.

Thank you.

Thank you for making them laugh. Thank you for all the crafts. Every single one. I promise they almost all made it to our home. Thank you for the endless jokes, gifts, and inside jokes.

Because of you, I got to listen to the giggles in the back seat all the way home.

Because of you, they couldn't wait to leave for the church on Sunday mornings.

Because of you, they're proud of what their parents do. (At least for now).

Because of you, the church became more than a place to suffer through as pastor's kids.

Because of you, they understand that rainbows mean everyone is welcome.

Because of you, they love to share with others what church they're a part of.

Because of you, my kids feel loved by God.

Thank you.

Saying Goodbye During a Pandemic

When I got the call about changing churches, my heart felt three things. First, I felt shock. I was not in any way prepared for or expecting this call. Second, I felt incredibly sad to leave Marysville. As you can see, a lot was going on in these five years and I'm not sure I had fully registered how much until I was asked to leave. Third, I felt curious about Edmonds. I wondered what God might be up to there and how I could support it.

As we navigated the appointment process, I kept my impending grief off to the side. Until it was official, I didn't want to figure out how to say goodbye to these incredible people. I found myself at our Board of Ordained Ministry interview week when COVID-19 entered the picture. We'd spent the previous Sunday sanitizing communion elements and avoiding shaking hands. As the news came in that more restrictions were coming, my colleagues and I scrambled to set up online worship and attend to our leaders at home in between meetings.

All the while, I held the fact that it was going to be announced that coming Sunday that I'd be leaving Marysville and going to Edmonds. Wait, what?! Should we announce this online? Should we wait until after this virus blows over? Little did we know what was about to unfold. I told our team and our District Superintendent I felt confident that we could make the announcement online in a kind and supportive way. Yes, it would be incredibly difficult, but we didn't have a choice. We were not allowed to gather in person.

I stood up in front of a nearly empty sanctuary on March 8 and looked at a camera lens and tried the best I possibly could to convey my heart to our people.

> "I acknowledge the oddness of sharing news like this in this format. Being a church family is about being incarnational. Together. In the flesh. Relational connectedness. Not only are we separated because of a community health concern, we are separated on a day we're getting news like this.
>
> It is not ideal. But it's where we are for the time being. And we will make the best of it.
>
> Last Sunday we talked about disruption in the wilderness. And here we are. Our church life together is feeling disrupted. A pastoral change. A virus keeping us away from each other. I know many of you are navigating new realities in your own family. We add in the national and global landscape in this season and it feels like...a lot.
>
> The Holy Spirit is indeed a bit of a wild child. Like a toddler, it's impossible to contain, constantly on the move, and doesn't listen to your direction. And the Holy Spirit is here, with us, embodied in our church family, even when we sit on couches in our own homes. Spirit waits for us to show up to our lives and pay attention.

It's here with comfort, challenge, and invitation, all the time.

In our personal wilderness journeys and our collective one, God is here. Jesus lives among us. The Spirit guides and comforts. We are people of deep faith. We hold fast to the truth of death and resurrection. In the midst of a disruptive wilderness, love is alive!

There are so many things I could say to you today, but because, one, we're not in person and two, because well, we all receive this news differently, I thought we could talk about a more intellectual thing that's helpful in this moment. Itinerancy. Then we'll talk about seed planting, how my family and I are doing with this news, some next steps, and a few things I need you to hear (even if you're not ready to hear them)."

I choked up a few times throughout the rest of the message. Especially when I named the reality that our friends new to United Methodism might not understand this process. No matter how much we talked about it in membership classes, it's not real until you watch it unfold. We named that it's okay to have whatever emotion this brings up. Anger, sadness, joy, acceptance, disappointment. We held a Facebook Live that evening so I could answer questions and we could be together.

Emails and texts poured in during the first week away from each other. I cried every day at some point, about something. In that first week, we received news that school would be moved online for at least six weeks. Our family was slowly losing our space to say goodbye and grieve in person. I grieved deeply that my children couldn't process this change with their friends.

Then there was this whole other experience that humanity shared: a global pandemic. We limited news consumption to a few headlines each day. Daily walks in the sunshine restored my fragile sanity.

Pajamas were the daily choice, along with high amounts of chocolate. Life slowed to an aching pace. It got slow enough that I could notice my shallow and tight breathing. I noticed the tears biting at my throat all day long. Fear, sadness, and disappointment took over my being while I reduced my daily intention to just get through the day.

I took comfort in memes, funny quarantine stories, and videos of people singing from Italian balconies. I drank water, slept in, watched "New Girl" and ate ice cream every night. I felt the guilt that we had financial resources, food, and a warm home. I wanted to do something to help someone but couldn't muster the energy to follow through. I quickly learned about collective trauma and how it drops us into a different way of being human.

In some small effort to make my outside existence match my internal reality, I started to pack. I started with a closet or under a bed. Each day, I filled up one garbage bag with things to give away. There's currently an entire corner of our living room filled with boxes and bags to be given away since collection sites are still closed. One afternoon, I found myself at church taking pictures off the wall and recycling unneeded files. I cried. I felt overwhelmed by the depth of gratitude I had for my time here. As I picked up each item, I welcomed all the feelings to come up. Gratitude, sadness, disappointment, anger, curiosity, and fear.

I tried to manage the grief, but it would not be corralled into my clearly defined box. It surprised me at every turn. The one place it was consistent was my afternoon walks in the sunshine. I cried every single walk for a month. My neighbors probably wondered if I was okay. I cried because I didn't know how to say goodbye to people I wasn't allowed to see. I wondered where the grief could go. It didn't have an outlet. At that point, the only option seemed to be down my cheeks while I walked around the neighborhood.

I reflected on past goodbyes and realized I've said goodbye to nine faith communities already. God, how is it that love keeps growing in me? How does it expand? I keep assuming it'll run out one day. And yet, here we go again. Somehow there's enough capacity in my heart to hold this grief, for it to one day heal and there will be still more room to hold the people of Edmonds. God, you are bizarre.

The days started to blur together. By the third week in quarantine, we'd found a new normal of late breakfasts, PJs all day, some online school work, screen time, outside play, and a daily walk. We figured out how to order groceries and pick them up to avoid going into the store. We video called, texted, and called our family. As global news turned dire, we committed to do our part to stay home. It was a bizarre season to hold the worldwide fear, our church transition, and our family's feelings as they shot around like a pinball machine.

As the days went by, I found myself needing an outlet for this grief. It had to go somewhere besides my cheeks. A few days after I started to name that invitation with my family and my coach, I got an email from a publishing company on March 25 that they wouldn't be saying yes to a book proposal I'd sent a month earlier. Oddly enough, my first reaction was relief. I'd been working on that book proposal for two years and my gut reaction was relief. My heart knew what I hadn't admitted out loud yet. That book wasn't the one that wanted to be written right now.

As I processed this news with Aaron, my parents and then Christianne, my book editor-spiritual director friend, an interesting new energy presented itself. I named that if I don't write or create in some simple way, I go numb and feel stuck. Christianne stated, "You are grieving, Jenny. I don't think you're avoiding the grief." I heard myself say, "I wonder if writing a book of some kind to my church is how I could grieve. I would sit down for a couple hours each day and sob my way through the book. The thought of letting them know in June that I wrote something and here's the Amazon link feels like a step of closure."

My soul came alive. Like a little kid on the playground shouting, "Pick me!" This was an invitation. It felt like there was a story to dig up. I heard my heart urgently saying, "You can't leave here until you tell this story. At least to yourself. Something important happened here. And you can't go to Edmonds with this story still inside."

The next morning, I opened my computer, started a new document, and thought about what I wanted to say to you, my church family. I wanted to say thank you. I wanted to tell you what you gave me, what I saw in you, and to celebrate what we learned together. I wanted to get you ready for your next leader.

I wanted to release you.

I had no idea it would also release me.

As I wrote each morning for the following month, new insights showed themselves. One day, early in the process, I wrote, "God, why are there so many tears just thinking about this project? Is it because my heart has been longing to do this? God, I'll do my best to make space for this journey. You do the rest. I trust you with this journey. It feels like too much on day one, but I trust your resurrection gift. I trust that if you take me into this, you'll see me through. You're already inside the pain I'm avoiding. Or denying. And I know you're on the other side of the grave too. God, I need you. Sustain and guide me."

Another morning I wrote, "I think I'm ready to enter into the Silence. The Listening. The Feeling. The Not-Avoiding. I'm continually astounded by how easy it is to avoid Loving Presence while loving other people. Even without this pandemic, I am in a painful and difficult season of life. My baby is going to kindergarten. I'm packing up our home. I'm saying goodbye to people I love. I'm reflecting on what I've learned in these five years. How I've changed. Deciding what I'll leave behind me and what goes with me."

As we approached Holy Week, I reckoned with the loss of liturgical markings. Our journey to the cross would be wildly different this year without embodied community, gathering in the sanctuary, the lilies, and Easter dresses. And yet, this is the Holy Week we needed during a pandemic.

God and I had a little conversation on Good Friday that went like this:

> **Me:** God, where are you?
>
> **God:** I'm right here with you.
>
> **Me:** I don't want to be here. I want Easter to be Easter. I want resurrection.
>
> **God:** Me too. The dying, then the rising. What are you still clutching to?

I went through the motions of Easter. I tried to concoct joy from thin air. But I was stuck in Holy Saturday. In the waiting and mourning. I preached that on Easter morning from our little office at the parsonage. I lit candles, plugged in a microphone, took a deep breath, and spoke to the back of my iPhone the invitations God had for us, even this Easter. Hope is here. Jesus is alive. It's still true, even if life felt like Holy Saturday.

A few days later, I noticed a curious pattern in quarantine life. I desperately wanted my church family to see my reality. My experience. I need to be seen and acknowledged. After talking with a dear friend, I saw it from a different angle. What I was asking was, "Can anything make this grief better? What if nothing can right now? It simply hurts." And what I was truly asking of my church family was, "please tell me all this mattered to you, too."

The isolation of quarantine was wreaking havoc on my goodbye process. I expected things from my church family they couldn't give. They were in trauma too and couldn't respond or engage as we might normally have done. I was trying to say goodbye to a church family who not only couldn't be together but was likely unable to be emotionally present to this grief of saying goodbye because of everything else going on. I intentionally released my expectations of how my church family could meet me in this process in this season. I would have to find another way to closure.

God and I had a conversation the next day:

 Me: "God, I want you to take all the grief away."

God: "Lean in, child. There are treasures here for you to uncover. I want my people to learn about it through you. Stay awake. Pay attention."

A day or two later, I read an essay by Glennon Doyle in her latest book, "Untamed." She tells the story of her sister's divorce. Glennon wanted to help but this pain was her sister's pain and she had to navigate it her way. All Glennon could do was sit outside her sister's bedroom door each night to make sure her sister knew she was with her.

I saw it. I've been trying to get my church to go with me on a journey that's a journey only I can make. Aaron can't go with me. My friends can't go with me. Only me. That's scary. It's a journey I didn't know I was still avoiding, even as I endlessly wrote each morning. The people around me have their own grief journeys to attend to, if they so choose. They can't know the uniqueness of mine. And wow, did that feel even more lonely.

I reached out to a few close friends and told them Glennon's story of sitting outside her sister's room. "I've been trying to take people on a journey that's not theirs to take. It's mine. Not everyone needs to know. But I need a few people to sit outside my door and remind me once in a while that you know." They each said yes.

With each essay I wrote, my heart felt lighter. The tears continued. I met with my therapist for our monthly visit, except it was online this time. We talked about tears and how I often labeled them as evidence of sadness. We talked about tears of gratitude. Then she said, "Jenny, your spirit feels delightful and happy. It sounds like you're thriving in the midst of great difficulty." We talked about the shimmering joy in my chest that co-existed with the anxiety and tension at times.

"Jenny, you're thriving. How does that feel." I replied, "Boring."

Curiously, I'm being invited to let go of the intensity of the last five years. I'm leaving past dysfunction behind. Granted, we've always got something so there will be plenty to unpack in the years to come. But this unique season of fear felt familiar. Comfortable, in a sense. I'm still attached to the story of how I used to be. And not because it was fun or thriving, but because it felt more comfortable to be deep in processing and painful growth than it felt to emerge and thrive. To shimmer, as my therapist named it.

How is it that thriving feels more vulnerable than suffering at times?

As I moved through the next couple of days, I experienced a few out-of-body observation moments where it felt like I could see what others see when they experience me. Those must be the things people compliment me on. But my experience, for so long, has been wildly different. And maybe I'm watching the story that used to define me slip through my fingers as I say goodbye to these people. It's more than saying goodbye to them. I'm saying goodbye to a part of me that no longer serves me. It doesn't fit here anymore.

Why is that sad? You'd think I'd be jumping for joy. Somehow in the complexity of growth, I also miss the me I'm setting down. I worked hard for her. She was my shield. And now I'm leaving her behind.

What's it like to say goodbye to your church during a pandemic? It's lonely. Isolating. Limited interaction leads to incorrect assumptions. Extra grace is required from all involved. It means noticing the way you loved me when it doesn't look like what I expected. It's a deep invitation to trust the love we shared for a season is the same love that holds me when we're disconnected. Saying goodbye during a pandemic is the ultimate act of trust.

And I choose to believe our time together mattered. To you. To me. To us as a body.

Thanks be to God!

A House Becomes a Home

Parsonage living is a unique animal. As a human navigating the already stressful season of life transition, it's helpful to know there's a house waiting for us. We don't have to shop, visit, or purchase a potential home. It's a relief to know we can give our full attention to helping our family acclimate, getting to know a new town and a new faith community.

And...you never know what you're going to get. Aaron and I grew up as pastor's kids so we know how this works. We made the best of leaky pipes, peeling linoleum, confusing floor plans, and faded furniture. We didn't know anything else. To this day, the only time I've gotten to choose where I lived was an apartment I shared with good college friends.

When we were first given the address of the Marysville parsonage, we scoured Google Earth to see photos from above. We zoomed in until the screen went blurry, looking for clues to our new life. All we saw were trees and a dark gray roof. Marysville leaders sent us a floor plan for our new home and we envisioned each room full of life and furniture.

After our introductory meeting with church leaders, Kim and Kass took us to the parsonage. Wesley napped in the car as we pulled up and parked. Lifting his carrier from the car, I looked to the right toward the house we'd been eyeing online for months. I admired the dense trees with light streaming through. I smiled and took a deep breath. *Our new home.* I positioned Wesley's carrier on my arm and took a few steps toward the front door. Kass called out, "Jenny over here."

We'd been looking at the wrong house.

Aaron and I caught each other's eyes and smiled. Oops. We sheepishly walked over to Kim and Kass as we talked about our new home. In the coming months, over fifty friends from church would paint, remodel, clean, plant, and prepare this home for us. *Our new home.*

One hot day in June, we arrived. I set Wesley down and he crawled around the empty living room. Isabella ran upstairs. We walked around, oriented ourselves to this new space, and imagined what might happen here. Over the next five years, this house became a home. We always knew it was temporary but it felt like ours.

We give thanks for BBQs in the backyard with friends laughing and enjoying warm summer days. We loved that the garage became Aaron's "Happy Camper Wood Shop." Well, at least three-quarters of the garage did. We give thanks for Aaron building us a camper in the driveway. We loved Trick or Treating in this neighborhood. We slowly figured out which houses gave the best candy! Beloved babysitters played and entertained our kids for our date nights. We give thanks for the well-worn pathways walked around the house while on long phone calls. We drew hopeful messages with chalk out front during quarantine. We loved walking our daughter to Pinewood Elementary for her first and second grade school years, a short ten minute walk away. Wesley learned to walk and ride a bike here. Our dog, Gracie, came to join us in this home.

This house was full of love, laughter, shouting and arguing. We grew in all the ways that mattered here. We welcomed new friends and talked for hours with old ones. This home was our sanctuary and we filled it well.

Soon, we'll take one box at a time out to a truck. This house will grow empty again. Voices will echo off the vacant walls. Tears will fall. Memories will be named one last time. I'll load the kids and dog in the van. I'll pretend I forgot something inside the house. I'll run in one last time, look around and smile.

God, we loved this home.

It sustained our family.

I rocked babies who somehow became kindergartners.

We watched too much Netflix.

We rocked on the backyard swing until the sun went down.

It's where I finally stood still.

This is the place I allowed life to love me back.

Thank you, church, for this home.

My People

Some people are so deeply enmeshed in our lives that it's hard to separate their existence from our own. These eight people are the ones I love most in the world. Their love for me is ridiculously consistent and deep. I love being loved by them.

Aaron

You are the unnamed presence in these pages. Your love for me is constant and fierce. Your commitment to our family enabled me to show up for this community. You listen to me, day in and day out. Calmly and patiently. Now the world has an inside glimpse into my brain and, sweet Jesus, now they know what a saint you are. Thank you for seeing my pain and not running. Thank you for how you loved this community. We've been partners in ministry for almost twenty years now and the last five were some of my favorites. I love you.

Isabella & Wesley

Being your mom is one of my favorite hats to wear. You teach me about love, patience, creativity, mood swings, and the value of a well-charged iPad. One day you'll read this book and understand some of what your mom was going through when we lived in Marysville. In a way, I got my joy here. I hope you felt it during our dance parties, puddle walks, and baking afternoons. Regardless of what was going on inside me at the moment, you got the best I had to give that day (most of the time!). Thank you for the snuggles, books, crafts, family game nights, and multiple goodnight hugs. Last of all, thank you for sharing me with our church family. God got to love lots of people through you two. What a gift. I love you.

My Parents

You two are saints. For almost four decades, you've been my lifeline. Consistent, present, and faithful. Thank you for every single phone call. The ones when I cried and you prayed for me. The ones when we laughed over your grandkids. The ones when you shared how life was changing in your world. The ones when you coached me through a tough leadership moment. The ones when you cared about the details of my life as only a parent can. If I could have personally requested two parents at birth, they would have been you two. I feel unconditionally loved, supported, and set free to continue becoming my full self in this world. I love being your daughter. I love you.

My Sister & Brothers

Thank you for the phone calls. For cheering me on. For trying to understand my world. Thank you for your grace and love. I adore our family and will continue to love you as best I can. I'll never forget that night on Mom & Dad's deck when someone decided it'd be awesome to play a truth game where we tell each other the hang-ups we see in each other. And one of you told me, "Jenny, not everything is something." Truth.

The three of you, more than anyone else in the world, know the part of me that I lost touch with over the years. The me who played in the backyard, built forts, colored at the kitchen table, and danced on the back deck. You knew the me I left behind when I thought I had to be someone else. I got to meet her again in recent years and I like her. Even if she was a little bossy to you guys. Sorry about that. I love you.

"Mom, I love you the most in this family."

— WESLEY

To 33-year-old Jenny

Oh sweet girl. There are some things I have to tell you. I see you packing up your home in Alaska, managing life with an infant and a preschooler while saying goodbye to the people who loved you unconditionally for fifteen years. You said yes to a new adventure with excitement and anticipation. Sure, there is anxiety dancing around the edges, but you are the consummate pro. No one will ever know, right? Just smile, be good and all would somehow be okay.

I wonder if you have an inkling of what is about to unfold. Maybe you wonder how you will keep it all together. Well, I have incredibly good and surprising news for you. You're about to have the time of your life. Fantastic new friends are awaiting you. You'll be challenged in all the best ways. You'll ask new questions that will change your life. Your new church family will teach you more than you teach them.

You're finally going to pull back the covers on the fear that's been running your life. That fear that you're not yet willing to admit is a problem. It will be tough. You'll cry in the silent corners of your life and then you will rise. You will be shocked at the resurrection that unfolds in your life. Oddly enough, you'll choose to tell people. Instead of hiding your imperfections, you will talk about them. You'll give others room to fall apart and rise with Christ, too. I wish you knew now how brave you choose to become. It's beautiful to watch.

There's a moment that happens that you could never imagine now. There comes a Holy Saturday during Holy Week where the church building is empty and you're going through deep transformation. You're about to tell the church about the panic attacks, the anxiety, and the resurrection. You're sitting in a chair in the sanctuary, reflecting on the table that's already decorated for Easter the next morning. You feel so alive and new and transformed, that this moment must be marked somehow. You stand up, walk toward the altar, which just the night before had represented Christ's grave. Spirit prompts you to lay down on the floor next to the table and let your fear die.

You do it. You lie on the ground and weep. *God, take this fear. Welcome it into your arms. I grieve it's passing in some ways. It's familiar and known. I'm not sure what will happen next. But I know I'll be okay.*

You eventually stand up, brush away the tears, and own the truth that you are becoming new. It happens in a moment and a lifetime. Fear will still be present in your life. You're human. But it increasingly has much less power over you. And that is a game-changer.

One day, you won't be changing diapers or cleaning up squashed peas on high chairs.

One day, your kids will run through a church building and declare it their home.

One day, your husband will start a wood shop and he'll love it.

One day, you'll realize what you curated for others ended up saving you.

One day, you'll look around Marysville and adore living there.

One day, you'll learn that sitting with your pain will shatter you.

One day, you'll get to put together a whole new life.

One day, the world will experience a pandemic and you'll have to move in the middle of it.

One day, you'll thank your church for being the container that held your transformation.

One day, you'll decide to say goodbye through a book.

It's unusual. But well, you're not really surprised, are you? That's how we roll.

Dear One, I love you.

I love who you are now at 33. I love who you become. All this change that's about to happen? It's good. It's deep. A becoming. And this next thing that's ahead after Marysville? You're going to have a blast. Because you'll be ready.

Love,

37-year-old Jenny

One Last Thank You

To the people of Marysville United Methodist Church,

I thought I was writing a book full of things I had to tell you.

It turns out, there's a deeper well of our experience that's easy to miss when we stop at our first read of a situation. The longer I get into this quarantine and the closer I get to walking out the door, a new reality has emerged underneath the one that was all about saying thank you for what you gave me.

Part of me died here. And it will change me for the rest of my life on earth.

That's what I'm trying to put into words.

I'm leaving Marysville a very different person from the one who drove into town on that last Saturday in June 2015. Because of the Great Pause of Pandemic, I'm just now beginning to wrap my soul around how much has unfolded in these past five years.

I recently spoke to my husband who so graciously listens as I process out loud. A lot. Really, he's a saint. I heard myself saying, "I'm feeling a bit dramatic. It's just a pandemic and a big life transition, it's not like someone died…"

Before he could nod or jump in or agree or share a counterpoint, I continued: "But part of me died here. I entered as a thirty-three-year-old woman expertly hiding a panic disorder and deep anxiety. I'm leaving an almost thirty-eight-year-old woman who wrestled, met, befriended, and released countless layers of pain, fear, and destructive ways of being."

Ahh. Maybe that's why I burst into tears anytime I think about what this place has meant to me.

This is the place I came alive. This is the place I got my freedom. You are the ones who served as my safety net without even knowing it. I had to find a way to say thank you. To tell you the part of the story you played. To show you one last time, this is one way it looks to follow Jesus. To stop hiding from Love. To open our clenched hands and receive grace. To lavish it upon everyone we know.

It's worth our freedom. To be fully alive.

Church, I love you.

Palms up,

Jenny

ACKNOWLEDGMENTS

Bishop & Cabinet: Thank you for sending me to Marysville. Thank you for sending me to Edmonds. I'm honored to serve alongside the people of this conference.

Brian: Thank you for flying to Seattle every month to share what you learned.

Mark: Thank you for telling me I have nothing to prove. I believe you now.

Dakota & Becky: Your love and care for our community means the world. I know they're in good hands.

Jane, David, Lynn, Kass, Colleen, Ed & Sherry: You caught the typos, corrected grammar and made a better experience for our readers.

Brianna: Your whole-hearted yes at the right moment made this profoundly better.

Bonnie: We have yet to have one face-to-face conversation yet your love for me and the people you champion is contagious.

My Bookwifery friends: Your deep belief in each other kept me moving forward when I most needed it.

My Instagram & Facebook family: I love sharing life with you. I wonder what we'll discover next!

My Palms Up Life crew: Two years later and I still love writing you every other week. Thank you for receiving the questions, stories, and love.

Melinda: Your listening heart moved me forward more than you know.

Rob: You named the title of this book and my heart resounded. Thank you.

Joe: Your belief in me and the work we're both called to brings me life. Honored to partner with you.

Jeremy: Your presence adds glorious laughter to my life. Thank you for bringing the party to every Zoom call and text thread.

Janelle: Thank you for your affirmation at key turning points when I didn't know how much I needed it.

Tanya: You told me to write the book and then rearranged your work to ensure I had time. You're incredible.

Kate: Thank you for volunteering to run the merch table years ago. Your faith in me is wild.

Anne: Thank you for saying yes at the coffee shop that day.

Deb: Your ability to listen to my heart and hear the rustlings of the Spirit astounds me.

Julia: Every other week I pull up your name in my phone and call you. Thank you for still answering three years later.

Christianne: Your leadership gift of creating spaces to listen to the questions of our hearts is pure gift.

Amy: You plainly named my future as if it wasn't even a question. Thank you.

Erin: Your presence and belief in me dance in the margins of these pages.

Smith family: Thank you for sharing Aaron with me. His love and spirit is a vessel for the holy. You raised him well.

Uncle Brian: Your joy at self-publishing was contagious. It's why you're holding this today.

Grandma & Grandpa: Your deep faith in Jesus is bearing fruit in ways you might not have imagined. I love you.

Beckett family: For better or worse, you're stuck with me. I miss you all. See you tonight on House Party.

Aaron, Isabella & Wesley: Thanks for giving me time to write these last two months. Where's the tape and markers? I'm ready to pack now.

Oh, yes. I said you could put a drawing in this book. Here you go!

ABOUT THE AUTHOR

Jenny Smith is a writing pastor in the United Methodist Church and serves churches in the Pacific Northwest. Jenny is married to Aaron and mom to Isabella and Wesley.
Learn more at jennysmithwrites.com.

facebook.com/jennysmithwrites
instagram.com/jennysmithwrites

Made in the USA
Monee, IL
07 August 2020